The Digital Critic

The Digital Critic

Literary Culture Online

edited by

Houman Barekat, Robert Barry
and David Winters

OR Books

New York · London

Published by OR Books, New York and London
Visit our website at www.orbooks.com

All rights information: rights@orbooks.com

First printing 2017

Cataloging-in-Publication data is available from the Library of Congress.
A catalog record for this book is available from the British Library.

ISBN 978-1-682190-76-0 paperback
ISBN 978-1-682190-77-7 e-book

Text design by Under|Over. Typeset by AarkMany Media, Chennai, India. Printed by BookMobile in the United States and CPI Books Ltd in the United Kingdom.

Table of Contents

Foreword

There is nothing remarkable in the act of opening a book to find a foreword and then an introduction. These prefatory forms are fundamental to the history of the book, providing a textual threshold to what follows. While both introduction and foreword are "at the service of a better reception for the text and a more pertinent reading of it," as the French critic Gérard Genette put it, each "vestibule" serves a different function. An introduction provides a rationale and a context, but a foreword, written by someone not involved in the book, more closely resembles a validating certificate.

There is something sweetly old-fashioned, then, about a foreword to a book on digital criticism. Isn't digital criticism the utopia from which mediating gatekeepers have been expelled, where expertise no longer entitles, and where free democratic debate has finally become possible? Isn't digital criticism the dystopia where corporate sponsored clickbait and listicles reign, and where all we want, and all we get, is more of what we already "like"?

Well, yes, and then no. The essays in this ground-breaking collection offer thoughtful and measured responses to all this, and more, from many points of view. *The Digital Critic* investigates everything from the "fake review phenomenon" to the "cultural logic of respon-siveness," from the capacity of online journalism to create a "truly deterritorialized esthetics" to its reliance on a "profusion of new gate-keepers." It considers long and short forms, paid and unpaid work, dedicated reader communities and Twitter-feed scrollers; it explores the dependence of online platforms on offline publications, and asks what a properly "born-online" criticism might look like.

One of the great virtues of this book is to remind us how much more there is to the online literary debate than "if you liked that, you'll love this." If the Internet has created a situation in which everyone is a critic, then the sheer volume of critical writing (or "content") itself calls for discrimination. And to do that we need to think about what we want from our critics.

The classic job description remains that given by Tobias Smollett in 1755, as he launched a new journal, the *Critical Review*. Convinced that criticism had become "venal and corrupt," he promised to revive its "true spirit." It soon transpired, however, that this spirit could only be defined by what his critics would *not* be or do. They were *not* "wretched hirelings."

> They have no connections to warp their integrity; they have no prejudices to influence their judgment; they will not pre-sume to decide upon the merits of a work in an arbitrary sentence unsupported by evidence; they will not condemn or extol, without having carefully perused the performance; they will not affect to draw odious comparisons, where there is no resemblance or relation; they will not invidiously seek to wrest the sense, misinterpret the meaning, or misquote the words of any author, who may fall under their inspec-tion; they will not exhibit a partial and unfair advantage of the beauties or blemishes of any production; they will not venture to criticize a translation, without understanding the original, or fill up the pages with long insipid transcripts:

In a word, they will not commend with reluctance, or *censure* with hesitation; they scorn to act as ministers of interest, faction, envy, or malevolence; they profess themselves indeed the enemies of dullness; but their favourite aim is to befriend merit.

I don't think it matters that Smollett himself never fulfilled this lofty brief, that he was better known for his rebarbative tongue, for giving and taking offence, and for knocking out reviews, and books, with only half an eye to scholarly standards. And I don't think it matters that the narrow confines of eighteenth-century London, where the professional (male, white, well-connected) "man of letters" was born, is a world away from the open-to-all digital landscape that this book so richly explores. If we've rightly grown suspicious of the authority of "universality" assumed by professional tastemakers, we should also be skeptical of the more recent authority of immediacy and self-expression. Thinking about what we won't accept from our critics is surely the first step toward identifying what we require. Befriending merit is not a bad place to start.

—*Kasia Boddy*

Cambridge, June 2017

Introduction

"I believe in life online," declared the Nigerian-American novelist and critic Teju Cole, in an interview with BOMB magazine in 2014, "the way a person in 1910 might believe in aviation, or a person in 1455 might believe in movable type: with excitement and apprehension." The same sense of ambivalence—of promise tempered by trepidation; of enthusiasm inflected with skepticism—pervades the essays in this collection.

The past fifteen or so years have seen an extraordinary flourishing of literary culture online, from blogs, forums, and social media comments to a rapid, and continuing, proliferation of online magazines and journals. Digital culture is currently changing every aspect of literature. In 2015, editors from three leading online literary reviews—*3:AM Magazine*, *Review 31*, and *Berfrois*—co-hosted a public seminar to discuss this ongoing sea change. It was from that event that this book was born.

The Digital Critic isn't a book about digital methods in literary criticism—such as new computational approaches like Franco Moretti's "distant reading"—but is instead about the changing conditions of criticism in a digital age. Has the Internet collapsed the distinction between serious critics and mere enthusiasts? How do the economics of online publishing affect critical culture? In a transient online environment, is there a future for long-form critical writing? Has the blogosphere stimulated the development of new kinds of literary and cultural theory? And to what extent have all of these transformations influenced contemporary literary fiction? These are just some of the pressing questions addressed in this collection.

Not everyone in the literary world is enthused by digital technology. In his recent memoir *The Art of the Publisher*, the influential Italian critic and publisher Roberto Calasso expressed pessimism about the future of the written word. He was responding to a widely-shared *New York Times* article, which approvingly portrayed the Internet as a "universal library," containing a copy not only of "every painting, photograph, film and piece of music," but also of "the billions of dead Web pages no longer online and the tens of millions of blog posts now gone." For Calasso, the prospect of a vast repository of undifferentiated material presents a threat not only to the gatekeeping role of the literary editor, but to literary culture as we know it. Ultimately, Calasso believes that solitude is integral to the literary experience. If digital technologies erode that solitude, something vital will have been lost:

> ...the secret, impenetrable, separate, discriminating, silent thought of the individual brain that reads has been replaced by society: an immense, all pervading brain consisting of all brains, whatever they are, provided they operate and speak through the Web. It is a concentrated babble that creates a new kind of unrelenting background noise, unfortunately crowded with meanings.... As for the world, it is canceled out, superfluous, in its mute, refractory extraneousness.

Although it's tempting to dismiss such fretting as backward-looking, it does speak to wider concerns about the implications of digitization for literary culture. Similar anxieties are alluded to in Tom McCarthy's fourth novel, *Satin Island*. McCarthy's narrator-protagonist is a cultural anthropologist hired to produce a "Great Report," a document which will encapsulate contemporary culture in all its mind-boggling multiplicity. The novel charts his uncertainty over how best to write this opus, an allegory for fiction-writing in general. At one point, he has a devastating epiphany: what if the entire digital record of human activity—emails, phone records, web pages—already amounts to the definitive account of contemporary life, leaving no point to further enquiry? "The truly terrifying thought," he reflects, "wasn't that the Great Report might be unwritable but—quite the opposite—that it had already been written, and that we, far from being its authors, were no more than actions and commands within its key-chains."

Whether imagined in terms of a "universal library," an "immense, all pervading brain," or a "Great Report," the problem of superabundance often dominates debates about online literary culture. Back in 2012, the editor of the *Times Literary Supplement*, Peter Stothard, caused a stir by claiming that the proliferation of book blogs posed a threat to critical standards. "If we prioritize unargued opinion over criticism," Stothard argued, "then I think literature will be harmed. It is wonderful that there are so many blogs and websites devoted to books, but to be a critic is to be importantly different" from those "sharing their own taste." "Not everyone's opinion is worth the same," he concluded.

A couple of rejoinders might be ventured here. The first is that online discourse provides opportunities to reinvent the very nature of criticism in ways that might enhance rather than diminish it, as Carl Wilson has suggested in his book, *Let's Talk About Love*:

> A more pluralistic criticism might put less stock in defending its choices and more in depicting its enjoyment, with all its

messiness and private soul tremors—to show what it is like for me to like it, and invite you to compare. This kind of exchange takes place sometimes on the Internet, and it would be fascinating to have more dialogic criticism: here is my story, what is yours?

But suppose we agree with Stothard on the "important difference" of the professional critic. As the *Los Angeles Times*' Richard Schickel persuasively puts it, "criticism—and its humble cousin, reviewing—is not a democratic activity. It is, or should be, an elite enterprise," drawing upon "disciplined taste, historical and theoretical knowledge and a fairly deep sense of the author's entire body of work." Here, it's worth pointing out that all of those criteria are now being met by some of the more rigorous online journals, many of whose contributors adhere to the standards supposedly under attack: they hold PhDs and lecture at universities; they publish novels with prestigious presses; they write for both online and traditional print publications—including the *TLS*. If online criticism were indeed limited to what Steve Wasserman, writing in the *Columbia Journalism Review*, has dismissively termed "book chat"—ephemeral, opinionated tittle-tattle of the Amazon reviews variety—perhaps we could agree that its net contribution to literary culture is small. But as the online world has grown more sophisticated, the caricature of the blogger as a dabbling dilettante seems something of a straw man.

Of course, members of the literary establishment were worrying about the democratization of critical response long before the Internet came along. The British novelist Martin Amis, in his foreword to *The War Against Cliché*, attributed the decline of criticism as a viable career during the 1980s and 90s to the egalitarian cultural shifts of the preceding decades:

It now seems clear that literary criticism was inherently doomed. Explicitly or otherwise it had based itself on a structure of echelons and hierarchies; it was about the talent elite. And the structure atomized as soon as the forces of democratization gave their next concerted push.

If the Internet's extraordinary effect on critical culture has made one thing clear, it is that, in the end, such oppositions are far too simplistic. Here, we're interested in the numerous subtleties and shades of gray that exist in between professionalism and amateurism, elitism and populism. For all the angst about the future of the written word, there's immense excitement, too: a revolution is occurring in literary life, made possible by new technology and networked culture. This book is an investigation of that revolution, of its pitfalls and possibilities.

—Houman Barekat, Robert Barry, and David Winters

The Upside of Being an Avatar: Critical Communities on the Web

Scott Esposito

Here's an observation that will surprise nobody: writers tend to be introverts. We network awkwardly and are drained after a few hours of enforced socialization. Anyone who's ever attended a writers' conference has witnessed abundant proof of this.

I believe there is a better way. Or if not a better way, at least *another* way. We are all increasingly taking advantage of this new alternative, and it is re-shaping the way we think and work.

Some necessary history: I started my first job in publishing in 2002 at a major American book distributor. It was an entry-level job entering ISBNs from purchase orders sent to us by bookstores. All day the purchase orders came in by fax and by mail (actual mail, not email), and all day I line-itemed ISBNs. Everything was run though a program called Cat's Pajamas that only operated in MS-DOS (there was an ASCII cat that wagged its tail). I became an absolute demon with the 10-key.

Data entry had its own unique thrills, but no matter how much I gamified my work it ultimately proved dull by mid-afternoon. One day a co-worker put me onto a website the likes of which I had never seen before. It was orange and its name was *Daily Kos*. It consisted simply of a series of brief, punchy observations on the latest political news, arranged vertically from newest to oldest. Throughout the day, new postings would appear at the top of the page. Kos was a snarky, savvy guy. I liked his tone and his politics. Soon I became addicted.

These were the years in which blogs were becoming the hot new thing online. People like Kos were exactly what the demoralized, disaffected American left was looking for. Keep in mind that 2002 was a very bad year: following the terrorist atrocities of September 11, 2001, George W. Bush was at stratospheric levels of popularity. He was using the "War on Terror" to justify a paleolithic domestic agenda, and in foreign affairs it was clear that we would invade Iraq. I have no doubt that this odious reality was the major reason why blogs caught on so compellingly as a medium. Hating on the Bush Administration was the killer app that made them a star. I broadened my Kos addiction with other blogs like *Talking Points Memo*, *Ezra Klein*, and *Eschaton*, as well as more obscure ones like *Digby*, *MyDD*, and *Poor Man*. With their slacker tone and their tendency to get the breaking news long before institutions like the Associated Press, they were absolutely gripping.

In these years I was just starting to publish my first reviews, and it occurred to me that if there were so many political blogs out there, there must be literary blogs too. With just a tiny bit of googling I found that, in fact, there were. Soon I was digging through sites like *The Reading Experience*, *Rake's Progress*, *The Elegant Variation*, and *Golden Rule Jones*. I lurked on these sites for months, and one day it occurred to me that I, too, could start my own blog. All you needed to do was pay a trivial sum for a basic Typepad account.

So in the summer of 2004 *Conversational Reading* was born. I began howling at the moon and a funny thing happened. Back in those days Typepad offered a basic stats page where you could see your pageviews, plus the twenty most recent referring links. Outside of a few conversations on message boards, this was my first ever inter-action with an audience for my writing. I was amazed to learn that such a thing as an audience for my writing even existed. Sometimes a blogger I knew on the Internet even wrote about me. Sometimes a major aggregator like del.icio.us linked me. Sometimes some guy whose moniker I could google left a comment on my website. All of this was visible to me.

I need to halt this story for a moment to point out what was not visible to me at that moment, but what was to play a very key role for me down the line: the lurkers in my audience. As I continued blogging, and as my reputation as a *blogger* grew, my audience would come to include the editors of major American book review sections, at least one editor at *The New Yorker*, writers and editors of pres-tigious literary journals, and other assorted individuals that I'm still discovering to this day. Eventually I would even get to know some of these people. This point deserves a little belaboring: simply because I started a blog and began tossing out opinions, I was able to become known to people of power and influence in my industry, some of whom down the line would be in a position to open doors for me. There are certainly few—if any—similarly powerful leveling mecha-nisms in the modern history of publishing, and I discovered this one purely by accident.

To return to our story: back in 2004 the Internet provided rudi-mentary ways to interact with my fellow bloggers. It's a little hard to imagine now, when any social media presence worth the name racks up dozens of interactions over the course of an average morning, but in 2004 it was a huge deal when another blogger responded to a post of mine, or when someone I knew on the Internet commented on my site. This maybe only happened once or twice a day at most. These responses were so exciting: gentle but forthright in their criticism, in-depth, sincere, honest, highly educated, very personal. It was a little like being in a great writing workshop, or having a mentor.

Eventually I began to orchestrate face-to-face meetings with people I'd been pinging back and forth with online, and here's the thing: the meetings almost always went spectacularly well. As in share-a-pitcher-of-beer-and-talk-books-all-night well. I began to see that this emergent social medium was a way to pre-select friends. I didn't have to go to an after-work mixer, I didn't have to do the coffee break at a conference—I could just wait for the right people to find my blog. I think this is because blogging tends to be a highly authentic, emotive medium; blogs thrive on personal opinion, so there's a huge incentive to showcase your true personality and real beliefs there. Through your presence on blogs and other social media, people can get to know you to a degree that's far more in-depth and honest than a first face-to-face meeting tends to be.

I immediately realized the immense potential here to drastically reduce the amount of my life I would have to spend at careerist get-togethers making enervating small-talk. All I had to do was keep blogging. The important thing for my nascent writing career was that these new relationships were becoming far more than just friendships: people I first established contact within the blog world were on their own paths toward being successful critics, editors at major magazines, authors, publishers, and so on. I've since written for these people. I've written books with them. They've made my work better in myriad ways. We've shared leads and propped each other up in times of stress. To this day, they're part of my inner circle. It's no exaggeration to say that my blog—much more so than my first job in publishing—has been the cornerstone of my life in letters.

That blog was my entry to a world that we all are increasingly living in.

Conversational Reading got started in 2004, several geologic epochs ago in Internet terms. At that point it was uncommon for a working writer—or anyone in particular—to have an Internet presence. Now things are completely different: virtually *everyone* has some sort of Internet presence on social media, and many of the purposes that blogs once served have been co-opted by lifestreaming sites like Twitter, Tumblr, Instagram, YouTube, and Facebook.

Nowadays I still blog, but my media of choice are Twitter and Facebook, which is largely how I meet people online. Both sites resemble blogs (and are often referred to as "microblogs"), but there are crucial differences. The biggest one is that your audience is no longer anonymous, and neither are you (many bloggers from the old era loved to use a pseudonym). Most social Web presences now include a photo—or, in fact, many, many photos—and it's hard to overstate how much this has changed the feel of operating on the social Web, now that you are able to see someone's face, their home, or their cat. The social Web is also much more instantaneous: you can count on immediate feedback to your postings; you can send text messages to people you have never actually met, and oftentimes they will respond within a few minutes.

The upshot is that it is now exponentially faster and easier to connect with people you don't already know, and these increases in immediacy and transparency have meant that a certain kind of manners have developed on social media. Simply put, there are now normalized, generally observed methods (one wants to say *rituals*) of meeting people online. They're now almost as routine as the cocktail mixer one-two punch of "Hi my name is . . . What do you do?" This tends to revolve around: a) first contact ("following" or "friending" someone); b) establishing commonalities ("liking" and/or commenting on content that you or they have shared online); c) light banter around these established subjects of discourse (this may include the beginnings of a professional relationship); and d) the eventual face-to-face meeting, frequently in the context of a business trip or conference.

This has had profound impacts on the life of the humble literary critic. Speaking personally, I make new contacts virtually every week, I've gotten jobs over social media, I've met booksellers who have become passionate champions of my work and my authors, I've discovered peers who have been assets to my writing. Because the Web is so transparent, I feel confident reaching out to people out of the blue: I know that if I do this they will immediately google me, where they'll see a picture of my face, lists of publications I've written for, people I've worked with, the titles of my books, and, of course, my blog. They will be able to scan this information and instantly reach a conclusion about my level of seriousness and "insiderness" that will probably result in a positive reply to my introduction.

Certainly mechanisms that have fulfilled similar social functions have existed in the past, but there are things about this new playing field that are genuinely new. First and foremost, social networks have flattened things. They have also removed so much of the anxiety and awkwardness of networking. This has enabled a whole new class of people who just don't do well in party-like situations to carve out a career. While some of these people probably would have found their way eventually, I think we have to appreciate the degree to which social media has enabled people who are poor networkers IRL to have a viable path forward. I think this is one crucial reason for the explosion of online communities among writers in the past decade. It is a more preferable way of fitting in. I, for one, far prefer social media to being forced to wander Book Expo America, or having to make small talk at an officious New York party. Whatever their flaws, online literary communities have never filled me with the death-wish conferred by even minor exposure to BEA.

Social media also allow a geographic range that would once have been prohibitively expensive: I've published my writing in print on four continents. I regularly interact with colleagues in Eastern Europe. I've done live stage interviews with people eight time zones away. I even comment occasionally in the Australian scene and have nontrivial contacts there who keep me up to date, despite my never having come closer to that continent than a trip I took to Thailand.

This globalization of instantaneous discourse has authentically allowed for new kinds of communities and esthetics. I need to mention that social networks are also the best method I've ever found of sharing and accumulating useful information as a critic. I don't mean the industry gossip about who's the latest to flame Jonathan Franzen; I mean vital, below-the-radar material that points you toward major writers that are being ignored by ninety-nine percent of the media and plug you in to interesting scenes that are in the midst of coalescing. For a critic determined to bypass industry hype and work with writers who will still be read fifty years from now, this information is worth its weight in gold. In addition to keeping your standards sky-high and broadening your sense of literature, it's hugely important for making those deep-in-the-stacks rediscoveries that critics live for. Most of my reading these days comes from seeing what's been energizing trusted sources online. A single, authentically blown-away tweet from someone whose taste I've come to admire can easily overpower a thousand words of turgid enthusiasm from some "old pro" phoning in his fourth review of the month.

This is the much ballyhooed capacity of social media to defeat mass media dinosaurs, and to an extent the hype is legit. I first learned about Knausgaard via social media. I learned about Ferrante that way, too, long before the *New York Times* would review her, not to mention so many other astonishing authors that major media outlets have never deigned to give a column-inch to. I've also kept current with the contemporary mainstream, despite having rarely cracked the august pages of the *New York Times Book Review* and its ilk in the past decade. Why bother, when a tweet will tell you everything you need to know about said review?

The immediacy and brevity imposed by social media have freed us to enter into a moderately idealized version of literary discourse that is just not possible in real life. Because it all takes place in a nonspace that you access with your keyboard, the online world removes the friction inherent in the act of performance art commonly referred to as a conversation. You lose a lot of the humanity online, but you're left with a purer grade of data.

In fact, there is so much data out there that we all must find our methods of triage against the gross abundance which pours down our timelines. We count our friends by the thousands. In just a few minutes on Twitter you might easily discover a dozen must-read books. For those of us who still read reviews, they are there by the ream. And don't even start with listicles! The online literary communities that have formed in the past decade are in many ways a response to this epochal glut. There is an esthetics of abundance here, an aspiration toward a Borgesian utopia—the joussiance of a book-lover who stares into a screen combining every worthy book ever written, all hyperlinked and lovingly annotated, with comments and chats and endless strings of thumbs-up from a gallery of cheering admirers—but also an esthetics of envy, of guilt, of overload, of attention-deficit, and of addiction.

We must ask ourselves: what are the consequences of a world where writers exist as disembodied data, shaped and curated by technological media moguls? The decimation of our gatekeepers has freed information, and what we now see online in the literary social media world is something akin to the perspective of the postindustrial financial markets. Within this free flow of information, we triage against data-glut by falling back on the semiotics of online relationships. We have begun to track individual books and authors like stocks. Who is up? Who is down? Who's peaked? Who is new? The raw information on which to base these judgments can be obtained through a handful of search boxes. I've watched so many people climb the ladder by making the same Facebook friendships and punching their tickets at a handful of websites. The information is all there—it's trivially easy to find out who someone is, who their friends are, who they've written for, and who reads those publications. With this great transparency, the non-space of our social networks has begun to define territory of its own: what once felt like a boundless free-for-all is beginning to shape itself into new forms of online territoriality. But this space doesn't exist in any physical way: we can't visit these places like the Beats could once visit City Lights and see the beating heart of their intellectual milieu. No, all of these spaces and connections exist strictly within our collective consciousness. They are only as real as our knowledge of one another and the countless hyperlinks stringing it all together.

Late in the summer of 2006, I boarded a plane bound for Mexico City. I had divested myself of ninety-five percent of my worldly belongings. All I had left was on the plane with me headed south.

That day was the beginning of nearly two consecutive years that I would spend living in various parts of Latin America. Not too long ago such a venture might have been career suicide, or at least career stasis, but this was exactly the opposite for me. I sometimes now refer to those years as "my MFA," because I provided for my expenses with a trace amount of freelance drudgery, leaving the rest of the time to read and write ravenously.

Much of this writing occurred in public on *Conversational Reading*, and my blog was a key part of finding my voice. For someone getting lots of rejections during this period, this blog helped keep me motivated, and it gave me an audience. What is more important to a developing writer than to sustain that kind of momentum? I kept a weekly column on my blog for these two years, and I would later sell some of the pieces I wrote; other pieces led directly to work with distinguished partners. Through my online reputation I also secured a few key assignments and connected with editors and mentors who pushed me toward more ambitious writing.

In addition to *Conversational Reading*, my other online venture during this time was *The Quarterly Conversation*, a quarterly web magazine of literary criticism. After the initial success of my blog, I had leveraged a number of its relationships into this production, which premiered in 2005 and was into its thirteenth issue by the time I returned to the United States (we published our forty-fifth issue in the fall of 2016). During my years abroad I had provided a home for developing writers like Garth Risk Hallberg, Sarah Weinman, Sam Sacks, John Lingan, and Lauren Elkin. I had also begun building professional relationships with myriad publicists, editors, authors, and translators, while getting a great sense of the contemporary literary landscape. I doubt I would have read many of my formative writers of that period if I hadn't first edited an enthusiastic review of their work.

I was fortunate to come of age as a writer alongside the tools that have made literary communities portable: *Conversational Reading* and *The Quarterly Conversation* were the two key ingredients in my emergence, and I had little problem keeping them both on the rails despite working on a tiny budget and traveling through wifi-unfriendly terrain like Tierra del Fuego, the Andes, Costa Rican jungles, and Guatemalan ruins, to name a few. This was all before the social Internet we know today existed, so these two websites were my vital means of connection: because of them, when I arrived back from my two years abroad, I wasn't a nobody who had vanished off the face of the Earth; rather, I was someone whose resources and reputation had been steadily growing, to the point that when I showed my face at Book Expo America in Los Angeles in summer 2008, it was as someone with the makings of a professional life and who was easily able to integrate into Bay Area literary culture later that year.

This was Web-powered freelance. What would have been my experience had I gotten an MFA? I would have read a lot of great books. I would have done a lot of writing, and it would have been read and critiqued by my peers, plus a few admired contemporary authors. I would have made connections, and I would have learned a little about working with agents and approaching commercial presses. I would have participated in a journal. On the downside, I would have accumulated a lot of debt, I wouldn't have gained the confidence of holding my act together for two years in foreign places, I wouldn't have traveled the world, and I wouldn't have developed the capacity to speak Spanish and read its literature in the original. I doubt I would have developed the level of book industry savvy and profile that I attained through my Web presence. Furthermore, although this is something I can't prove, I have the suspicion that I would have left an MFA as a fiction writer instead of an essayist/critic. I absolutely tie my calling to the time I spent abroad and the years I spent learning my trade by writing on the Web. I imagine the MFA would have injected me with the influence of the so-called program writing that Mark McGurl has associated with the university's dominance over postwar American literature, and here we see a vital alternative that the social Web has opened for English-language writers.

Another vital difference: an MFA would have taken me toward a job within the knotty groves of academe, instead of my freelance lifestyle. Here again we see deep synchrony. To freelance one must be comfortable as an outsider, highly motivated and self-starting, eager to hustle up opportunities, and, most of all, prolific. This is precisely what it takes to blog, and, by extension, to seize the opportunities on the social networks.

Because I've kept my distance from the academic world, the social Web is my foundation—the logic of the blog sits deep within my prose style, and the Web has remained key to my esthetic: so many of my main literary relationships occur primarily via screens. It is important to note how durable these contacts have been. Many collaborations I first instigated in the 2004-05 era are still intact, and most people who were participating in these early Web communities have gone on to have viable literary careers. These possibilities are now magnified extraordinarily. With the immediacy of text messaging, email, and Skype (to say nothing of social media), it is now possible to have something approximating an IRL friendship with a person who lives thousands of miles away. We possess the means to form deep esthetic schools unbounded by geographic location, and we are seeing the first generation of writers to harness these powers to create truly de-territorialized literary esthetics. This potential is visible in *The Quarterly Conversation*: from its earliest days the project was unbounded by national borders, and our community has been key to the growing reception of Eastern European authors (László Krasznahorkai), Latin American authors (César Aira, Horacio Castellanos Moya), and an Australian (Gerald Murnane). We have also nurtured the careers of critics living from Argentina to the United States to France to Australia. Whereas literary schools were once built around a scene in a particular city, they can now operate worldwide by coalescing around nodes in cyberspace. In fact, I would go farther: this is increasingly becoming the norm. Many of the projects I most admire and collaborate with are distributed in exactly this way. In fact, the book this essay appears in is a perfect example of such de-territorialized collaboration.

There is no doubt that the social Web has been hugely influential for all of the reasons I've discussed here, but we must also be aware of its limitations. I offer the following juxtaposition to demonstrate this point.

Few would disagree that the VIDA count has had a profound impact on curing gender disparities in literary criticism. It demonstrates that a group with a resonant and easily quantifiable message can quickly and economically seize a social media narrative. In just a few years, VIDA's campaign has increased awareness of the intense gender disparities in leading magazines and literary journals, and it has had an admirable amount of success in changing practices and producing greater equality. It has done this with very little money and an all-volunteer staff.

One might wonder, however, how critical memes that require more nuance, induce less reflexive agreement, and are more difficult to embody in easily sharable, graphic statistics might fare. One example is the loose network of translated literature advocates that has managed to lodge a few star authors on the bestseller lists and create a general sense of guilt among those who read only English-language writing. On one hand, it has been a success: everyone now quotes the three percent statistic (even though there's little actual data to back it up); the media-share for translated authors has grown significantly; the independent bookseller community has taken up the cause with an admirable passion; the work of translators is now much more visible and appreciated; and there are more translations published. But on the other hand: the fraction of translated books published each year remains miniscule; few superstar publishers or literary icons have come out to champion the cause; the quality of criticism of translated titles in the popular media generally remains atrocious; and translators themselves are still widely marginalized and poorly paid by many presses. Clearly, a lot of translation has improved in the past decade—many attest that it is in the best place it has ever been—and key to this success is the de-territorialized community of critics, publishers, authors, booksellers, and translators that has coalesced online. But in order to push things into a higher echelon, more work is clearly necessary. This is the general critique of Web advocacy: it is possible to get the message out to a certain group, but pushing beyond that is hard and frustrating. With the VIDA count—where the main point was to reach editors in a position to change practices—there was little need to move beyond the particular audience most easily reached. Leveraging public opinion was not important because virtually no one opposed the idea that more female writers should be published and discussed. But with translation—which has consolidated its niche audience and now wants more—pushing to a broader level of awareness is essential to further growth.

Web communities can only go so far. To put this into concrete terms: I buy a lot of books, and even more books are mailed to me by publishers hoping I will review them. I frequently post cover photos of books I want to promote to my audience. Invariably these images rack up a large number of "likes" on Facebook. However, perhaps ninety percent of those "likes" are from the same individuals. There is considerable evidence here of hardening esthetics, but much less evidence that people beyond a narrow sphere of adherents are falling in love with the books I want them to read. Thus the limitations for pushing translation to a broader audience online purely with Web-based tools. But now consider this: I also do perhaps fifteen public events each year that highlight new work from authors I appreciate, and here the case is precisely the opposite. There are always those same few people who attend almost every single one of my events, but the great majority of attendees are people I have never seen before in my life. Here we have the longed-for "viral" effect in a decidedly old media production: people beyond my immediate sphere of influence are coming to my event, hearing my message, and propagating it to others. Another name for this is "word of mouth," which even in an Internet-based society cannot be beat as a tool for reaching new audiences.

Web-only enterprises have been traditionally weak at building institutions because they are poor at projecting power beyond the Web. They are potent tools for discovering the unacknowledged allies within a given network, and they share information among these people like wildfire, but they have a difficult time moving past this point. Translated literature, for instance, has largely made its significant inroads because the Web advocacy has been backed by many new translation presses that have sprung up around the United States in the past decade, as well as by bookstores across the country that have pushed these books and the critics who have managed to place them in the pages of old media titans. These are physical institutions, occupying physical space, with people producing material objects in the real world. Their range of possibilities is far more energetic than a website, which fundamentally must passively wait in the hope of being accessed by the correct person.

That is the power of a network: for those in the know, we are all the correct person, and we have an unquenchable thirst to keep accessing the lives of our fellow networkees. This desire to keep up with the lives of people we care about is a part of our basic humanity, and it is correct that this practice is now swerving along the curve of the technological zeitgeist. But it is worthwhile to ask: what does the infrastructure want, and what does it *not* want? In a world increasingly flattened and universalized into a nowhere of electrons, where do today's silences sit, and how can we ever find them? The social Web is an enabling place because it is built out of visible, legible, transparent gestures. But what about the things that don't fit into that regime, what about the Web's silences? Where do they reside, and how can they be found? For someone who is interested in producing extraordinary work and moving the culture forward, the answers to these questions will be at least as important as figuring out how to successfully navigate our increasingly virtual literary communities.

The Oeuvre Is the Soul: Confessions of a 21st-Century Hack

Jonathon Sturgeon

The philosopher Boris Groys posits that the "body of work" of the artist or writer has come to replace his soul as the "potentially immortal part of the Self." The idea is uncomplicated; it shimmers with the sweat of self-evidence. Even the religious writers among us would rather be judged by the St. Peter of literary perpetuity; to be read often and after death is the only afterlife. What else explains the arrival of a six-volume automation of the self by an ex-Protestant Norwegian demigod? Or the poem-novels of Ben Lerner, whose metafiction nods to the theories of Charles Olson, the poet-theorist of proprioception? Wasn't it Olson's *Proprioception*, an apocryphal gospel for all things auto-, that taught us to see the corpus, the material body of work, as the self?

These may be extreme cases, but, if we take the argument of William James in *The Varieties of Religious Experience*, it's the examples of "religious extravagance," of eccentricities of the soul, that illuminate the whole. Nor are these the only examples; shades of Groys' pronouncement can be found in the majority of contemporary writing, which is stricken with the mania of identification. Even if no one wonders any longer what contemporary literature is (or could be), we can at least sense that we aren't wading in the world of the storyteller or the anti-self, of Benjamin's Leskov or the Yeatsian daimon. Anyway, is the prose fiction of Knausgaard or Lerner really so extreme? There are other cases.

On October 1st, 2014, I unwittingly became a literary hack. Or, if I knew what I was getting into, I felt I had little choice in the matter. After six months spent abroad in London, where I wrote only two essays—an accepted but still unpublished diary entry about my time as a pawnbroker in Indiana, and an obituary for Alain Resnais—I returned to New York, where, because of a fortuitous series of house-sitting gigs, I was able to survive for another four months. Near the end of this stretch, at what you might reasonably call the zero-hour, I was hired as a literary editor on the recommendation of a gifted critic and essayist, a friend I preferred not to disappoint. It was not lost on me, at the time, that I had been rescued by a small band of editors and artists. It left me believing, after months of austerity living, that less would always be enough.

In the years before, I edited the back-of-book criticism section for an underrated literary magazine, a print monthly that had declined, by then, in frequency (it ran out of cash). My work there was slow and satisfying, bolstered by a young, brilliant editor who has since taken to obscurity. I still admire, in some respects, the younger critic I was in those days, but I can admit that I had become sheltered from the medialogical concerns of a literary culture that had migrated, bit by bit, to the Internet.

But I wanted to write. And my new role demanded that I produce seven posts a week for an online publication with an unfortunate name. Still, it had something of a literary following, if one was devoted, like much of the literary Internet, to bookchat. It turned out that, during my years of neglect, online literary culture had been overwhelmed by informational givens, by lists, by news items about literary happenings, by think pieces, and by the occasional spiritless interview. My original intention was to square my instinct for self-preservation with my gift for self-sabotage. I would appear to acquiesce to literary culture (and the demands of my job), but I would do so on my own terms. In the first month, I wrote reviews of Marilynne Robinson's *Lila*, Nell Zink's *The Wallcreeper*, and Claudia Rankine's *Citizen*. This, I felt, was dutiful, even if these pieces appeared alongside a list of "10 Plague Novels That Will Not Help You Deal with the Ebola Virus."

Before I knew it, I was producing content at speed; I could no longer remember what I had written the day before. After the first year, it occurred to me that I was responsible for more than 150,000 words and hundreds of posts (of varying quality). Rightly, I still believe, I was penetrated by loneliness. There couldn't be another writer alive so indentured to daily literary concerns. In an act of pure fantasy, I aligned myself with the image of the authentic literary hack, with Twain and Poe. Prodded by the ghost of the Protestant work ethic, I had offered myself to countless books that few cared to read. It was undeniable: my tattered, proletarianized soul had been colonized by online publishing, and I was moving worstward, against the opportunism of the "fail better" ethos. Instead, I was failing worse. My personal slogan, chanted at the end of a seven-day work week: "Work hard. Go out on bottom."

There were moments of resistance. In time, I learned to leverage book excerpts from willing publishers (all of them) to buy myself editorial time. Though I had no freelance budget, I provided space for willing interns and assistants to write about new books, on the grounds that I could rescue my section by editing them far beyond the standards of online writing. Whether they are now better writers, I have no idea, but at least they learned not to rely on marketing language when reviewing literary fiction. And, against the pull of traffic, I covered territory mostly abandoned by others: left-leaning politics, academic works of literary quality, translated fiction, and poetry.

And, like any old laborer emerging into low-grade consciousness, I saw my struggle elsewhere. In online writing, the depletion of editorial time is a function of a blind reliance on advertising revenue. I admit there is nothing new about this observation. What we might call the monetization of hermeneutics is by now a fact of the Internet. But no cultural form is afflicted by this fact more than literary criticism, which requires a surfeit of time to produce (over and above cultural "forms"). Is it any wonder that TV critics are now replacing literary and film writers at the pittance of remaining online outlets? It takes hours and days to read a novel. It takes thirty minutes to watch an episode of television.

The reduction of editorial time, make no mistake, is taking its toll on offline publishing—on books, for instance. The emergence of co-authored literary fiction has curiously been seen as a mode of vanguardism, but it is just as likely the result of an inflation of literary aspiration butting heads with a lack of time (two Word documents are better than one). Along these lines, genre fiction, which relies on readymade grotesques and prepackaged forms, is especially vulnerable to speed. In the last year, we've seen hordes of nerds gathering in hotels to group-write fantasy novels, as well as highly publicized crowdsourced science fiction. Even the ghostwriter has been mobilized and naturalized in order to make time for literary production. The highest grossing debut novel of all time was written in 2014 by a ghostwriter in service to a YouTube megastar. If this doesn't bother you now, it will, when, in the future, you discover that you've read or reviewed a "literary fiction" produced by an author whose name isn't on the book. Soon even pseudonyms will be resigned to history.

All literary writing, in other words, could tend toward automation, and by this I don't mean the workmanlike fortitude that allows Nell Zink to write several novels in a year, or that spurs Knausgaard to produce twenty pages in a day. Though, on the other hand, it's not obvious to me that either case is separated from the exigencies of literary production. In any case, what's at risk is more than the fate of one literary hack.

If the body of work of the writer is his soul, what is there to say about the soul of the daily literary critic? I'm trying to tell you that my soul became a hash of listicles and poorly edited interviews, yes, alongside a handful of respectable reviews and one or two quality essays. But I'm also arguing that, in a small way, my soul is a harbinger of souls to come. The reduction of editorial time, the automation of writing, the elimination of working memory (and, in aggregate, historical memory): all of these are accelerated by online writing, at least when it is set to the speed of advertising demand. But now that this demand is crumbling, there is no guarantee that daily or even weekly literary critics will survive. For better, or probably worse, there will be at least one less soul, body of work, or self—whatever you want to call it—for literary posterity to deny or redeem.

Isolation, Solitude, Loneliness and the Composition of Long-Form Fiction

Will Self

In 1938 Cyril Connolly, the critic, published a book called *Enemies of Promise*. It's a kind of manual about how to write a good novel. Some unkind people say that that's something Connolly himself conspicuously failed to manage though he was pretty good at telling other people how to do it. I actually think that Connolly was a great man and a great man of letters. His greatness, though, was very much a function of the time he lived in, and of the kind of culture that surrounded him. What are the enemies of promise? There are eight enemies of promise. The most famous of them is perhaps caught by the most famous apothegm which says "there is no more somber enemy of good art than the pram in the hall." And there are seven other enemies of good art: sex, drink, success, public success, conversation, daydreaming, politics, and what Connolly terms "writing substitutes," by which he means exactly what he got up to during most of his professional career—book reviewing and various kinds of journalism. He might even have regarded academia as something of a substitute for proper writing.

I would dissent. I don't know that I've necessarily produced "good" art over the last quarter of a century but I've produced something, and I haven't been deflected in my course by sex—I wish there'd been rather more of it but, I can't say that the pursuit of it has really hampered my writing, I would say it's rather fed into it. Drink and drugs? Well, I don't believe that the road of excess leads to the palace of wisdom, and I always tell young people who know of my own history that a given drug experience might be interesting but repeating it a thousand times is pretty bloody boring. Also, in my own case at least, I can honestly say that drink hasn't been the enemy of my promise. Public success? No. On the whole I've enjoyed success and I've found it easier to get up in the morning and write fiction knowing that it would be published and it would very likely be read, so I would slightly dissent from that. I think a lot of the difficulty which people experience while writing long-form fiction is because they know it never will be read, which is a terrible thing. So I dissent from Connolly on the question of success. Politics? Don't get it really. I suppose in the 1930s, with the kind of savage political currents that were running around, if you fell victim to fascism or Marxism it could easily scramble up your fictive capabilities, but we live in rather more ridiculous times: at any rate, we often live in a kind of privileged apolitical bubble that seems removed from the real business of our world. So politics hasn't been a big issue at all. Daydreaming? I thought daydreaming was part of writing fiction? I really went into the business in order to daydream. So I don't get that one either. The two I really do accept though, utterly, are conversation and the pram in the hall.

Conversation and the pram in the hall. They absolutely militate against the isolation that is key in my view to producing long-form fiction of any seriousness or integrity. In 1949, Connolly's justly-celebrated arts, literary, and political review, *Horizon*, closed, and Connolly again rose to the occasion with an apothegm: "It is closing time in the gardens of the West." Meaning that from now on the artist will be judged for the resonance of his solitude, and the quality of his despair. I think he thought that was kind of grim, but that to me sounds light. The kind of rubric I have followed in my career has always been against the enemies of promise. Now why am I harping on Connolly? Because my very dear friend Cressida, who is his daughter, is here this evening.[1] Cressida has been the midwife of my isolation for the last quarter-century: for twenty-five years she has lent me a small cottage in the Devon town of Dartmouth and that's where I go when I'm working on the most intensive phase of my novels, which is really the end. I need to tell you a little bit of my working methodology because it relates to this question of isolation.

By definition a writer needs to write alone. You cannot write while you're having a conversation. In the early '90s when I was a young tyro I was friendly with a lot of the artists who became known as the Young British Artists, people like Damien Hirst and Tracey Emin. It always used to really piss me off that they would go out all night getting bladdered and then the next day all they had to do was put a kebab on a table or get their assistants to pickle a shark. And they could do it while chatting to people as well. How unlike the life of the writer, which by definition has to be in isolation. When I start to write a draft of a novel I need to be completely alone. I don't write all day when I'm working on first drafts, I write in the mornings. I start when I get up, usually very early. Why? Solitude, silence, only having the contents of your own mind present to you. And also, slightly strangely, I think there's a very close connection between dreams and fiction. I think there's something oneiric about fiction: it is dream-like. The interesting thing about dreams is that we do tend to suspend disbelief in them. Fiction is inherently preposterous. It's telling lies, it's making things up. I find it's a lot easier to make things up while completely alone very early in the morning.

I'll knock off at lunch. But by the time I get to the middle of a book I start working in the afternoon as well. In the afternoon, I start

_____

[1] This is an abridged version of a lecture given to students at Brunel University, London, on 16 March 2016.

re-writing the book from the beginning. So it's a bit like painting the Forth Road Bridge: I start, I'm still writing the first draft going forward from the middle, and I'm writing the second draft from the beginning at the same time. And when I get to the end I start working on the third draft as I'm still working on the second draft, and so forth. When I get to what I call the "painting the Forth Bridge stage," I need complete isolation for as long as it takes. Because I find that something happens to the text once you've got a certain proportion of words together. The text seems to acquire the lineaments of a psyche of its own. It starts to seem to think for itself. But you can't really hear it thinking for itself if children are bothering you with their needless requests to be fed and educated and have clothes bought for them. You just can't hear the text calling to you with its little voice saying that *it* needs to be fed, *it* needs to be fed imaginatively and it needs to be responded to. It seems to me that to hear your characters, or allow these inchoate characters to acquire embodiment, you need to only enjoy their company, not the company of others. Connolly was right: conversation is a killer, because it's louder than the voices of the characters that you're trying to create. Yeats said that "poetry is the social act of the solitary man," and I think the same applies to prose fiction. But really the solitary man has a kind of society in his mind at the same time, and indeed the fictive process is bringing that internal colloquy into full voice.

So that's how I have worked over the years and I have found that it has required considerable amounts of isolation. Dartmouth in Devon isn't that isolated. I've also spent a lot of time in the Orkney Islands or did up until about 2005, and that is pretty isolated. I'd also go to provincial towns: I'm fortunate to be affluent enough that I can go to a provincial city somewhere in the British Isles, rent a room and just write there. Because it's completely isolated. There's no possibility of me being interrupted or interfered with. There is actually a kind of literature of literary solitude itself. There's a whole kind of sub-genre of fiction about men and women wondering around provincial cities by themselves for no apparent reason, and that's because they're written by writers who are writing about what they know, which is themselves wandering around provincial cities with no apparent motivation other than writing books. So a writer like WG Sebald definitely qualifies for that. Kazu Ishiguro wrote an entire novel that was quite clearly about him writing a novel.

The social act of the solitary man, a room of one's own and fifty guineas a year: all of these have been touted as prerequisites for the fictive process. But if writing is the social act of the solitary man, then what else is? And the answer is: reading. Reading is the social act of the solitary woman or man as well. It requires solitude. I think we take reading for granted. Reading isn't like speech—we're not hard-wired for it. It's a technology that we have acquired over millennia. And if you look at the history of syllabaries and logo-syllabaries, the history of how the alphabet came into being, you can see how remarkably complex and involved and socio-culturally relative a skill reading is. My favorite reading anecdote is the encounter between Augustine of Hippo and Bishop Ambrose in the fourth century: the bishop was in his garden in Milan and Saint Augustine came upon him and Bishop Ambrose was reading silently, and Augustine was profoundly shocked. He had never seen a man read a book not aloud. Almost all reading was aloud at that time. Mostly because, of course, people weren't literate. But also because the model of reading was a monk reading to his brothers or a nun reading to her sisters at meal-times or during religious services. That's what reading was. People didn't read alone. Reading alone and reading in solitude by definition is something that we've come to acquire as a skill and we now can all do it pretty well. You can sit on a crowded bus and become absorbed in a text, the sounds will mute, you'll become unaware of where you are and you will put vast amounts of cognitive activity into your visu-alization of what the writer is trying to convey to you. The long-form text, the novel, is a kind of meeting ground between two imagina-tions that agree together to spin an evanescent world into being. But what's going to happen to this act in the wired world? What is going to happen to this quality of solitude that we require as both writers and readers? In a world in which we're all permanently connected and permanently in conversation with each other?

I'm absolutely confident that the codex is going to pass out of use within the lifetime of younger people in this room now. If you look back at the history of the codex, and you look back at the history of literature, it doesn't take very long before you realize that alterations in the technology of print production have had profound effects on the kind of literary forms with which people have been engaged. Marshall McLuhan is perhaps the most percipient theorist of the emergent communications landscape. Recall that his book *Understanding Media*, in which he coined the expressions "the global village" and "the medium is the message," was published in 1964. Yet it reads as fresh as paint. The novel really wasn't around much at all before the mechanization of the hand press in the early 1800s. You can point to all sorts of aspects—you might want to wax Weberian and look at the rise of capitalism, you might want to think about those kinds of inputs and social and economic forces—but I think the technological substratum is strong enough to provide a kind of robust causality for the form. Particularly when you note that we moved from triple-decker novels in the mid-nineteenth century – which are a function of serialization in relatively small-run magazine publications—to single-volume novels with the inception of web-fed offset printing in the 1880s and 90s.

I came of age as a writer in the mid-1980s, and I now realize that that was in fact the apogee, the high point of literary culture, the culture of the codex. What I didn't realize was how short-lived that culture had in fact been. I've pointed to web-fed offset printing, which created a revolution for all sorts of print, creating all sorts of new forms and genres. But there are other factors in play in the twentieth century as well that are equally important: for instance, the educational reforms of the National Liberal government under Asquith in the early 1900s that led to universal literacy. It's very difficult to imagine the literary culture of the twentieth century without everybody being able to read. Universal literacy, printing, distribution systems, perfect binding, the invention of the paperback book: you could arguably say that the literary culture I came to know in 1985 was only in fact forty or fifty years old, but of course it seemed immemorial to me. All successful cultures believe that their values are supreme. You might notice how the West is absolutely convinced that its values should prevail worldwide. I daresay the Romans felt that their peculiar brand of slave-kleptocracy should dominate the world. No surprise that the culture of the codex should have not only believed that it was superior to all other forms of cultural dissemination, but also that it had been there forever. And I think that's why people are finding it so hard to realize that we are now past the apex and traveling down the other side.

If you wander around Brunel University, what you will see is an educational institution struggling to cope with the inception of bidirectional digital media. What you see is a lot of digital immigrants trying to teach digital natives. And a lot of digital immigrants have what McLuhan would call Gutenberg minds, minds that are formed by the idea of the codex. You'll all remember Hannibal Lecter's memory palace. It's a common idea in Greek culture, and actually mnemonic systems of all kinds were incredibly popular in pre-literate or quasi-literate cultures because it was necessary to remember vast amounts of data. In a way, everybody with a Gutenberg mind still has a memory palace, has a personal canon, has learned to commit a lot of data to memory. A key idea of what it is to be a cultured person is to have that personal database and be able to relate it and coordinate it to the idea of the canonical. You become a kind of individual scholar or a learned or cultured person by the way in which your individual mini-canon slots into the big canon. However, the inception of bidirectional digital media seems to do away with the necessity of that form of transmission. And with the necessity that the individual mind hold that much data within it. What you see around the university are a lot of signs up saying "F is for Fail" and a lot of signs warning students against plagiarism because it's so easy to do now that almost all human knowledge is digitized. We run a course for English students here called Reading Resilience. The title says it all. Often in Reading Resilience lectures I'll say to the students "try and read for five minutes with your phone off, and then the next day do ten, and then the next day do fifteen."

But I don't think bidirectional digital media is making people stupider—on the contrary, I think it is making people smarter in certain ways—but it is changing the world we live in. What we find is that it's staying isolated with a text that students find particularly difficult. What they also find difficult, because they no longer live within the intellectual culture that gave rise to a book, is staying within the text intellectually. Now those of us who have Gutenberg minds, we read a book and we expect to stay in the text. Not only that, we expect the text to be self-explanatory. We might get up and consult a dictionary, but we probably won't. We probably will just keep reading in the hope that the word we don't get will be explained by its presence in a different context, and that's how we'll learn a new word. But what do you do when you're reading in a medium where you simply have to touch the word and a little definition pops up? Or you touch the word and a little multimedia presentation comes onto your screen, showing the word enacted by skilled thespians? The text has ceased to contain you: it's ceased to be an isolation module. It's ceased to be the form that replicates your own unitary consciousness. The novel in particular has evolved to be internally self-explanatory. That's how the form operates: it mixes the diegetic and the memetic in order to tell you everything you need to know without getting up from your chair: you just turn the pages. But that's not what bidirectional digital media is like at all.

So what's going to happen? I never said the novel would die; I think it's too exciting an art form to die. I don't think that's a likelihood at all. But I think it has entered a kind of care home, where it's being looked after. It's being looked after quite well—it's in one of those slightly upmarket private care homes, not one of those ghastly local authority ones where you sit in a puddle of your own cold urine for hours. And that care home is the Academy. And the form the care takes is manifold: if you look at the history of literary criticism it tells you a lot about our attitude towards narrative in general, and the novel specifically.

In the nineteenth century people believed in God. God made us in his image. A bit like characters in a novel. And then god died. But before god died, he told us everything that would happen to human-kind— beginning, middle, and end—because God saw us *sub specie aeternitatis*—from the prospect of infinity—a bit like a novelist, who knows the end as well as the beginning. Then God died and novel-ists, for a brief while, became God. No really! If you look back now on twentieth century literary criticism, Connolly and *Horizon* had massive historic and political importance, particularly during the war. But I would argue that's because of the death of God, and because of the artist coming to occupy, for a brief and blissful period, a kind of godlike status. And what we saw as a result of this godlike status was the erection of an enormous critical apparatus in the arts and human-ities, in which people studied these novels, commented on them, developed theoretics in respect of them, from the Frankfurt School— Walter Benjamin, Adorno, people like that. Even in the contempo-rary era, you find a situation in academia in which people's perfection of their understanding of a particular theoretic rubric with which to interpret the meaning of the novel (or other art forms) is their profes-sional expertise. In British universities you actually meet academics who call themselves Derrideans, or Althusserians, or deconstruction-ists. Is it possible to imagine this state of affairs ever coming about without the particular intellectual history that we've run through? I somewhat doubt it.

So exaggerated did the apparatus of critical interpretation of lit-erary works become that it engendered its own kind of reaction. So you have Barthes and the "death of the author." A bit like Darwin and

God; Barthes and his relationship to the author. Kill the author, he says, let's just regard the text a bit like the world once God is dead. We can then be objective about the world, and we can be objective about the text. But you can also see it as a function of the entire tradition of western metaphysics kind of running out of steam in the middle of the twentieth century. What are those poor philosophers and metaphysicians going to do if they can't say anything about the world? Oh, I know: we'll start treating novels as if they were worlds. Because previously we were treating authors and writers as if they were gods but we've killed them . . . but we've still got the novels and they'll be our words and we'll philosophize about these little mini-worlds. And that's what you often find: people in English departments philosophizing about texts. I'm not criticizing it: that's just what we're up to.

Literary criticism is not an enemy of promise. I mean, Connolly seems to think if you write *too much* literary criticism, it might stop you writing novels, but he doesn't think the entire arena of literary criticism is an unwholesome distraction. I'm not so sure about Creative Writing though. When I first came to teach here, I went to an MA Creative Writing session—Celia Brayfield was running it. They sit around and read a bit from their work and everybody in the room comments on it, gives instantaneous feedback. It came round to me, I gave my feedback and Celia said to me "No Will, this is the positive feedback session." I said "Celia that *was* my positive feedback." But it's not the positive or the negative nature of the feedback that matters. It's the bringing a generation of writers into being, apparently, nourished only by conversation, and not isolation. That's what worries me.

The problem for me with Creative Writing is that it encourages people to imagine that they can pursue a writing life in some kind of comity with other people. It's a bit like being a visual artist: you could have people into the studio and sort of muck about in that way. The other problem for me is that it suggests that it's something that can be taught, whereas it seems to me that the novelist is the supreme autodidact. Because just as the text itself needs to explain everything about itself within its own parameters, so the individual writer needs to be capable of bootstrapping themselves into the competence necessary to convey whatever it is that they want to convey. That's not something that you can be taught to do. It's something you've got to teach yourself to do. And then there's the third main problem, which is that the entire culture for which these aspirant writers are being educated is winking out of existence even as they are becoming qualified, in some sense, to do it. The spectacle, as far as I can see, is of novelists who cannot earn a living by writing their own novels, training other people to become novelists, who will not be able to make a living except by teaching *other* people to become novelists—and so on. And indeed, even in the last five to ten years, the arena of Creative Writing has become professionalized to the extent that it is now required to have a doctorate in Creative Writing in order to teach Creative Writing at a university. The numbers of Creative Writing students keep on going up, but it's a bit like joining the Sealed Knot or some kind of historical preservation society that goes round dressing up in costumes and re-enacting battles on the weekend, because what this really represents is the terminal moraine at the end of the great cool glacier of literary production.

When I start talking in these terms which people find rather apocalyptic about the end of the codex and therefore a radical change in these kinds of artistic and literary forms, people start to look very uneasy. As well they might, because the Gutenberg mind is a real phenomenon. I had dinner with Simon Schaffer, who is Professor of the History of Science at Cambridge, a few weeks ago. He made one really interesting comment as we were parting. He said, "The big thing that liberal humanists don't understand is that human nature has no history." It really doesn't. But this particular kind of Gutenberg mind *does* have a history. It definitely does date in some ways from the early modern era. Students came to interview me about Shakespeare's five-hundredth anniversary just before this lecture and I reminded them that the famous critic Harold Bloom felt that Shakey had invented the modern personality as it is. And now we're seeing its demise in an important way. And I often wonder, if the novel is the form of the unitary and isolated consciousness, whether in fact the novel is such a good thing after all, or such a great art form after all? Is it not an art form that has underwritten a certain kind of separation and distance between people?

One of the reasons I think there's been very little resistance to this epochal technological transformation from analog to digital is because we were very much softened up for it in the twentieth century. McLuhan wrote *Understanding Media* in 1964. In it he referred to something he calls the unified electrical field, and if you read the text it sounds very like the web. But he's not talking about the web, he's talking about the nexus of telecommunications technologies that were existent in the 1950s. When you think about it, the bidirectionality, the ubiquity, the broadcasting capability, they were all there in a latent form. And so we've kind of been conditioned to the idea already. We've already experienced lots of these kind of phenomena— cognitive, phenomenological, and social phenomena as warped by bidirectional digital media—in embryonic form. But the new media landscape is of a completely different order to the unified electrical field. And I believe its effects on human consciousness will be radical. Its effects on the Gutenberg mind will be to blow it away altogether.

One of the things that led me into all of this was writing fiction in isolation itself. The last six or seven years I've been preoccupied with writing a trilogy that unites the changes in human psychopathology, human technology, and human warfare throughout the twentieth century. When I look at the inception of modernist writing in the twentieth century which wants to kind of do away with narrative, which borrows montage from film, and which often involves really quite abrupt elisions and cuts between one individual psyche and another, I wonder whether or not the modernists were not pointing the direction or the way towards a new kind of consciousness, or rather a new *old* kind of consciousness. The philosopher

John Gray made the observation that we can hypothesize that human consciousness arose at some point in our evolutionary history as a byproduct of language acquisition, and that would seem very strongly to privilege our culture of the text and the book. Gray goes on to say that perhaps in the future consciousness will be a function of media, not of language. I actually think we're already living in that era.

In late 2014, ISIS began to upload videos of beheadings onto the World Wide Web, and there was a kind of spasm in the body politic. I recall Philip Hammond, Defence Secretary under the Coalition, being interviewed on television. When asked what his response was, he said that because of the *videos*, not the beheadings, Britain would be spending £2.2 billion on a new naval base in Bahrain, and that this represented a further twenty-year commitment to military involvement in that region. That was all in response to an *image*. The videos were not even authenticated at this point. Again you might say "Yeah, *Ace in the Hole*, Kirk Douglas, we've seen this all in the twentieth century, you're saying nothing new." It's the scale of it; it's the febrility of it; it's the interconnectedness of it. And really it's the idea that in fact linguistic consciousness may have been a sidetrack. It may be that the image-based consciousness is what we really have.

How do I feel? Really excited. There's a Chinese proverb that's also a threat: may you live in interesting times. I don't find it to be a threat at all. Am I disappointed to have spent all this time working on an art form that I see melting before my very eyes? No. Not particularly. Things change. I *am* depressed about the isolation though. No really. Twenty years in solitary confinement. It may even have been more than twenty years. The friendships I could have nurtured. The relationships that might have been more successful if I hadn't been shut up in the room. The fresh air I could have breathed! I have grown old shackled to the form of the novel; it's been my ball and chain. That is a bit depressing. But the actual transformation, the actual dying away of the novel form? You may think I've been rather critical of the teaching of Creative Writing. I *am* critical with respect to the novel and how it came about in this kind of atmosphere of isolation and how this consciousness was formed in a reciprocal relationship with the form itself. But these Creative Writing students are gonna take us somewhere else. They'll invent new forms in relation to new technologies of print dissemination. I find the students here adorable: bright, engaged, and alive in a very exciting world that is undergoing a great deal of change. I won't come out with the whole hoary old adage that they have a lot to teach us, but I think as pedagogues we perhaps need to consider that we may not have that much to teach them anymore.

Fragmentation and Aggregation: The Future of Criticism?

Luke Neima

Robert Coover anticipated a generation's worth of anxiety about literature in the digital age when his 1992 essay "The End of Books" ran in the *New York Times*. "The print medium is a doomed and outdated technology," he wrote. Digitization "both absorbs and totally displaces" what came before. According to Coover, the whole enterprise of writing fiction was at risk—how could the traditional novel compete with the books that would be written online, using hypertext to link a reader one way and then another in an infinitely expandable web of narratives, a Borgesian "green-limned garden of multiple forking paths"? It wasn't just writers who would be affected, but critics too:

> Hypertext is truly a new and unique environment. Artists who work there must be read there. And they will probably be judged there as well: criticism, like fiction, is moving off the page and on line, and it is itself susceptible to continuous changes of mind and text.

Books, it turns out, have not moved entirely off the page (at least not yet). E-books have been holding steady at around thirty percent of market share in the publishing industry over the past five years; and the industry as a whole has just posted its largest profits since pre-digital times. Despite decades of "Death of the Book" headlines, the print industry that surrounds literature shows no sign of flagging.

Coover proved far more prescient in his prophecy for literary criticism, which has been heavily digitized—along with much of contemporary cultural discourse. This is because forums for literary criticism and comment have long been reliant on larger platforms, whether this be newspapers, magazines, or editions of collected essays. It is the organization of these kinds of media platforms that have been most transformed (and disrupted) by digitization.

In his series of essays on technological analysis, *Breaking Smart*, Venkatesh Rao calls the year 2000 the dawn of a new era of soft technology: "after written language and money, software is only the third major soft technology to appear in human civilization." Rao argues that the fluid nature of development and communication provided by software means a move away from the dominant trend of hierarchal, top-down structuring of industry. For him, we are at the dawn of a lateral, networked and pluralistic age of production. This has very much been the case when it comes to news media. In an age of declining print circulation, newspapers and magazines have been forced to redefine themselves online, diversifying their offerings and business models.

Effectively, the number and range of platforms by which literature can be criticized, discussed, and debated has grown exponentially in just a few years. This new landscape has resulted in a shift not only in the way criticism is written and read, but in the role it plays in the larger literary climate.

For much of the last century, the triad of author, critic, and reader dominated the way literature was produced and consumed. An author's work was subject to a series of critical filters before it was even made available to a reader: in the first instance, an editor and publisher weighed and judged whether it merited publication, along the way editing and shaping the text to suit what they understood the market to want. Once in print, the work was assessed by an elite of privileged connoisseurs—often full-time, professional critics at newspapers and magazines—whose approbation (or disapprobation) would have a definite impact on the number of readers seeking the book out at bookstores and libraries. Readers' opinions hardly entered this model at all: readers were passive recipients of decisions made by the publishing and media industry.

While these traditional roles still exist, the shift in literary criticism from print to digital has fundamentally altered this model of interaction. The hierarchal system of texts being assessed and approved by cultural authorities has been superseded in many cases by a horizontal network of lay readers, who can now take the decision of what should be published and read into their own hands. Reviews and criticism in the traditional form are being supplemented, and to some extent supplanted, by endless streams of user-generated Amazon and Goodreads reviews, book discussions on forums like Reddit, Voat, 4chan and Medium, by book blogs, and by an ever-evolving list of social networks.

Authors too can bypass the traditional publishing model by looking online. There are websites for writers to publish electronic drafts of their work, sites devoted to self-publishing, and an array of crowd-funding services. Kindle Direct Publishing dominates this market, taking Word documents and feeding them directly into Amazon's store. Independently published authors pose significant competition to traditional publishers in terms of market-share—and have also proved enormously successful with readers. More than half of Amazon's Top 100 Best Selling e-books in 2015 were self-published.

What does this all mean for the roles of critic, author, and reader? One striking consequences of digitization is how the boundaries between these roles have dissolved—for instance, there are now more readers writing reviews of books than critics. Furthermore, authors, in search of publicity in an ever more diversified marketplace, must now step into critical roles to promote their latest books, or to offer reader reviews. Additionally, critical platforms seek out authors to write criticism rather than lesser-known critics simply because their credentials—putting out a book with a traditional publisher—are so much easier for readers to recognize.

The hard and fast distinctions between critic, author, and reader do not exist anymore. A few foolhardy individuals are determined to fill all three roles at once, as when prominent historian Orlando Figes donned a number of fake identities on Amazon to say his own work "leaves the reader awed, humbled, yet uplifted" and to criticize his closest competitors as being "hard to follow" and even outright "awful"; or when crime writer R.J. Ellory claimed that reading his book would "touch your soul" and that his rivals were writing "an endless parade of same-old-same-old Police procedurals."

This blurring of roles and its consequent shifting between voices has had a knock-on effect on the language of criticism. Professional critics, like writer-critics and reader-critics (and even sock-puppeting authors like Figes and Ellory), increasingly tend towards a personal register in literary analysis. *The New York Times* books section runs headlines on "Literary Bromances," "Rough Reads," and "Day Drinking" with authors. *BuzzFeed* reviewers regularly call books "game-changing," "dreamy," and "mind-blowing." The common thread running through all of modern criticism is unfaltering positivity.

In large part, this change of tone is due to the use of social media as the main way of distributing such criticism—the "writerly" or "readerly" voice is more accessible than a dryly academic one when it's excerpted for use on Twitter or Facebook. The desire to attract traffic—and to be read—ultimately shapes the language and style of criticism as a whole. As in any syllogistic process we haven't entirely lost the old model—we still revere star critics like James Wood and Michiko Kakutani as we once revered Lionel Trilling and F.R. Leavis—but the role of a critic-qua-critic is no longer as recognizably meaningful (or even necessary).

Everyone's a critic, but what happens when everyone's a published critic? What criticism do you actually bother to read? This problem is amplified by the ever-growing number of books that come out each year. It's not just the multiplicity of critical articles that pose the problem, it's the myriad forums, journals, blogs, and reviews where one might read them. As Coover puts it in his essay, "how do you move around in infinity without getting lost?"

The difficulty in knowing what is worth reading has given rise to a new critical tool: the aggregator. In a literary forum, aggregation means selecting the best literary reading from around the web and making this available as a list of links in one place by critically assessing a range of literary or critical posts to save readers time. Aggregators range in style from sites that only aggregate, to those that supplement aggregation with more substantive content, and to social media hubs like Facebook and Twitter, where links are aggregated from the people and pages you choose to follow.

The multiplicity of platforms that comes as a consequence of digitization makes aggregation necessary. It is a powerful new critical tool to deal with the sheer unorganized quantity of literary content now available online. This is criticism in terms of what might be worth a reader's attention: aggregators simplify the daunting task of trying to stay on top of the Internet's vast offerings by doing some of the work, piling all relevant articles in one place.

Relevance is determined by the curator: the nytimes.com intersperses the live feed of articles by their authors with those from the *Atlantic*, Associated Press, the *Globe and Mail* and many others. The

Paris Review's round-ups push back to the book pages at the New York *Times*, the *New Yorker*, and the *Guardian*; while *Arts & Letters Daily* aggregates from over a hundred different newspapers, magazines, and reviews. The style of article that each site chooses to feature becomes part of the branded identity of the site itself. In this way we see a shift away from publishing primary material to a mixture of content creation and content curation, revealing the drive to become a trusted literary portal, a reader's guide to the rest of the web.

Aggregation in literary forums isn't limited to lists of outbound links. For instance, the *Paris Review* aggregates book recommendations fortnightly by getting their in-house staff to blog about what they're reading. *The Millions* aggregates a "top ten books" list by watching what their readers buy on Amazon and *Electric Literature* asks authors to recommend short stories and novel excerpts that have had a personal impact on them.

What does all this aggregation mean for the business of publishing? On the face of it, linking away from your website to content elsewhere, or passing off lists of work done by others as your brand's curated product, both seem problematic. It's a stark move away from the traditional model of critical production, in which a newspaper or magazine proudly features only the content for which it is responsible. The shift represents another fundamental change brought with digitization, a change toward a networked structure of businesses rather than a range of discrete competitors.

Jeremy Rifkin forecasts the economic impact that this kind of digitization has in his book *The Third Industrial Revolution*: "The partial shift from markets to networks establishes a different business orientation. The adversarial relationship between sellers and buyers is replaced by a collaborative relationship between suppliers and users . . . adding value to the network doesn't depreciate ones own stock, but, rather, appreciates everyone's holdings as equal nodes in a common endeavor." When one website links to an article posted by another, both profit. The linker becomes a curator of media and a portal to literary news, while the linked site gets an instant boost in traffic. In the networked model the distinction between content creator and content providers disappears. Often, the most successful approach is to do both.

This shift to increasingly networked forms of criticism both demonstrates and promotes the collapse of the traditional triadic critical hierarchy, cultivating a new horizontality of voice and authority. The upshot is a permanent change in tone—critical media is now only rarely couched in the point of view of the prescriptive expert. Instead charm, friendliness, and "irresistibility" reign. There's still space for deep thinking and insight, but the distance between high and low has been reduced.

While the quality and originality of some of the content in networked literary culture may be questionable, the ease of communication and feedback that comes with it promotes discussion, diversity, and debate. One of the most positive results is perhaps how quickly and easily expressions of literary taste and value can be challenged. When *Esquire* compiled a list of "The 80 Best Books Every Man Should Read" that included only one female author, the critical response was swift and brutal (best represented by Rebecca Solnit's withering essay in LitHub). Esquire responded quickly and penitently, by releasing a new list, "80 Books Every Person Should Read," compiled by "eight female literary powerhouses, from Michiko Kakutani to Anna Holmes to Roxane Gay." After decades in the thrall of curmudgeonly canon-makers like Harold Bloom, a horizontal literary culture offers a welcome opportunity to challenge overweening assertions of authority, resulting in an open, inclusive—if occasionally fractious—climate.

While the effort of carving out a new niche underlies the launch of most new critical platforms online, the means by which we access these platforms and the media they provide has consolidated around a few key social media outlets.

Aggregation itself is an increasingly fractured and difficult to navigate field. Facebook, in particular, has taken advantage of this by positioning itself as the aggregator of all aggregators. Users have become accustomed to being fed recommendations from friends. In the past years, Facebook has placed an increasing emphasis on businesses having pages, which then feed content to their followers. Because Facebook is so ubiquitous and easy to use, this has often supplanted businesses' use of bookmarks, email newsletters, or RSS feeds, and at the same time has allowed Facebook to monetize its business model.

The Facebook posts of businesses are only shown to about ten percent of their followers—unless they pay for a Facebook advert, or a "boost." On the one hand, this offers marketers a set of unprecedented advertising tools, in terms of demographic specificity and reach, on the other hand, it puts smaller outlets at a significant disadvantage, separating them from followers who have voluntarily signed up for their offerings.

In April 2016, Facebook took their primacy in organizing content to a new level by launching an "Instant Articles" feature, aimed at destroying the bridge between its platform and the platform of others altogether. "Instant Articles" are ostensibly intended to make the experience of reading on mobile devices "faster and richer on Facebook," making article load times up to ten times quicker. Not incidentally, however, the feature also keeps users on Facebook itself rather than directing them away to third parties, even though they are reading content produced by a diverse set of independent publications.

Apple followed suit quickly with Apple News—an aggregator of newspapers and magazines that streams directly onto Apple phones and tablets. Literary forums can hardly hope to compete against the advances made by big tech, and it remains to be seen what effect the monopolization of reading platforms will have on critical writing itself. If the remaining divisions between social media and critical platforms are successfully dissolved, what distinction will remain between a review written as a Facebook post and one on the book pages of *The Washington Post*? The drive towards monopolized aggregation puts readers at a further remove from those they are reading, and further fragments an already fissiparous field.

The role of the critic—and the nature of criticism—is in a state of flux as never before. Just as the boundaries between reader, writer, and critic dissolve, so too do those between the literary text, the critical text, and the advertisement—and so too do those boundaries dissolve between critical media, literary media, and social media. The ongoing evolution of form goes hand in hand with changing content. The move from hierarchal to networked models of criticism promotes an altogether different style of writing, rewarding suspense and comprehensibility over complexity of thought.

All the approaches to aggregation listed above embed critical fragmentation into the infrastructure of modern critical media. From the outset we're faced with a network of opinion rather than a set of discrete choices—and the fragmentation of criticism has only just begun.

The Digital Critic as Public Critic: Open Source, Paywalls, and the Nature of Criticism

Lauren Elkin

In early 2014, the *New York Times* journalist Nicholas Kristof wrote an op-ed called "Professors, We Need You!" "Some of the smartest thinkers on problems at home and around the world are university professors," he said, "but most of them just don't matter in today's great debates." This is in part a problem of context; American anti-intellectualism (and this is true in Britain as well) marginalizes education, prioritizing plainspokenness and common sense. But worse, Kristof said, academics have "marginalized themselves" through a "culture that glorifies arcane unintelligibility while disdaining impact and audience."

In *The New Yorker,* Joshua Rothman responded to Kristof's piece, begging to differ. The problem is not self-marginalization, he wrote; it's that "the system that produces and consumes academic knowledge is changing, and, in the process, making academic work more marginal." Rothman suggests that Kristof's perspective is blighted by his being a journalist, "because journalism, which is in the midst of its own transformation, is moving in a populist direction," adapting to new pressures to drive traffic and to create new forms of addressing the public that will enable them to "interact"—all this in a mad dash to monetize content ("content," not "writing"). Journalists are

plying their trade in a new atmosphere of "economic and technological developments having to do with subscription models, revenue
streams, apps, and devices." Rothman condemns academic culture
for being as "knotty and strange, remote and insular, technical and
specialized, forbidding and clannish" as the writing it produces. But
the answer, he writes, is not to ask academics to write differently, or
more accessibly. Rather, "[i]f academic writing is to become expansive again," he argues, "academia will probably have to expand first."
Rothman doesn't provide a clear way for this to occur, so let me do
so, in two words: open access.

In spite of the pressures that the Internet creates to rack up hits and
turn them into advertising dollars, it seems to me that the Internet is
a place where these two forms of engagement might come together.
Academic writing would improve if academics were writing for more
people, if they could begin to understand that their work matters beyond
their own sphere, if they could let go of whatever makes them write the
way they do, and, most importantly, if they could be sure that their work
would be received and respected. There is something that happens to
writing when writers are aware of their audience and when they can
picture their work being received. Academics are used to anticipating
the critiques of their colleagues, through the process of peer review.
But what if they were no longer writing only for their peers, but for
a curious, interested lay reader? What if—I know this is heady stuff—
what if our research actually began to *matter* beyond our disciplines?

For this to happen we need, quite literally, to open the door to
the ivory tower. And digital criticism can act as a lever. Much of
what is happening in academia is cordoned off from those critics and
readers outside of the university, in the form of subscription-based
journals and databases charging exorbitant fees for access. If you don't
have a university affiliation, or a friend with one, it's nearly impossible
to read the scholarship in those journals without a trip to a research
library. This presents a problem for academics and civilians alike: for
scholarship to intervene in the culture, it has to be accessible. The

responsibility of the non-academic critic to know what has been said, and to intervene in that conversation, is blocked without access *to* that conversation. Likewise, the conversations taking place behind that paywall will be transformed in ways that will only help scholarship if it is being read by a larger public. If research is going to have any impact beyond the academy, it cannot be limited to those with subscriptions to university libraries. When even Kanye West has complained about the price of textbooks, you know you've got a problem. But you also have a solution: Kanye West is paying attention to textbooks! We have an audience, if only we can reach it.

But it goes the other way, too. Paywalls barring literary criticism from view make non-academic writing as obscure and unreachable as academic writing. Someone recently asked me why I didn't review Chris Kraus's *I Love Dick* when it was republished in the UK. I did, I said. For the *Times Literary Supplement*. Oh, my friend said. I can't afford to subscribe to that. This is simply the world we live in: if it happens behind a paywall, it may as well not happen at all. And since I've taken the time out of my research and teaching schedule to write the review for a "mainstream" publication, I can't tell you how disheartening it is to think it went largely unread except by the subscribers of the *TLS*. That sentence would have been a little ridiculous fifteen years ago. Of course a review in the *TLS* would only be read by its subscribers, and those who bought it on the newsstand! But we're living in a new paradigm of content that is widely available beyond the traditional subscription model.

I'm not here to offer a new business model for academic or mainstream publishing; that's way outside my purview. Instead I want to suggest that this is not a separate problem from that of academic writing walling itself off; these examples are part of a larger issue, to do with the instrumentalization of research and writing alike, regardless of its readability, by neoliberal market forces. We have to make our words accessible, to tear down the false binaries that keep researchers and critics apart, and to keep academic research relevant.

This may sometimes mean making our work available for free on our personal websites, as I've sometimes done with my *TLS* reviews after the paper's been published, at a respectful delay. Later in 2014, Steven Pinker wrote a piece for the *Chronicle of Higher Education* on why academic writing is so unreadable. When I first went looking for Pinker's article, I found it on the *Chronicle's* website, behind a paywall. It looked like this:

"Why Academics Stink at Writing"
By Steven Pinker September 26, 2014

Together with wearing earth tones, driving Priuses, and having a foreign policy, the most conspicuous trait of the American professoriate may be the prose style called academese. An editorial cartoon by Tom Toles shows a bearded academic at his desk. . .

Luckily I have an affiliation that allows me to go to my university's library webpage, log on to Lexis-Nexis, and look up the rest of the article. But if I didn't have an affiliation, I wouldn't have been able to go and read the piece at all.

Pinker's article is a thorough analysis of how academic writing sucks (signposting, hedging, inability to conceive of ideas in a non-abstract way), and why, in a section that marshals cognitive psychology to make its case. But the final reason Pinker cites is that academia doesn't teach or reward good writing. There is simply no incentive to produce clear, well-written research. "Enough already," he says. "Our indifference to how we share the fruits of our intellectual labors is a betrayal of our calling to enhance the spread of knowledge."

Except! Googling a little further I found Pinker made his article open access, hosting it on his own website. I didn't need my affiliation after all! Academics have attempted this as well, posting their publications on academia.edu and other similar sites. But journals object to this practice: if you're making your work available for free, why should anyone pay for their journals to read the same work? At least one journal to which I've recently contributed informed me of this when they sent the proofs of my piece. So this is the way it works: if I write for a journal like this, only people who subscribe to that journal or go looking for it at the library will read my piece.

The issue applies as well to journals that are only available in print. There is still a degree of prestige attached to being published in, for example, the print issue of the literary magazine *Granta,* rather than on its website (though that is, of course, an impressive place to be published in its own right). This, I imagine, is because there is a finite amount of space in the print journal, whereas there is simply more room to publish on the Internet; certain pieces which are enhanced by being on the Internet, as well, will appear there. But the fact is that if you're published on *Granta's* website instead of the print journal, far more people are going to read your work. And being read is its own form of prestige.

The reasons for research to be open access, and for articles to be released from behind their paywalls, run the gamut from the ethical (research should be available to all who wish to consult it) to the pragmatic (perhaps it will lead to new, less exploitative, business models). A subscription to a database of books and journals like JSTOR costs, for a medium-sized university, a one-time payment of $85,000. None of this money goes to the authors or editors of the journals. JSTOR, a not-for-profit organization, uses these funds to run their operation and has not raised their rates since 1997. Nevertheless, their service has come to stand for a certain kind of debate about the availability of scholarly material. In 2011 the computer programmer Aaron Swartz was indicted for downloading several million articles from the site, though he did not actually disseminate them. The Federal government went after him with the full force of the law anyway, threatening him with 35-50 years in prison and a million dollar fine. John Naughton speculated in *The Guardian* that this drove Swartz to his suicide in

2013. Why did the Feds pursue Swartz so mercilessly, Naughton asks? It's not like he hacked into a bank, or shared state secrets. He merely downloaded academic articles.

I remember, around the time of Swartz's death, having an exchange with someone on a friend's Facebook wall about JSTOR and the open access debate. Why would anyone who wasn't an academic *want* to read those articles? It's my job to read them and I can barely be bothered. Was it so that libraries wouldn't have to pay an arm and a leg to subscribe to these databases? Or so "independent" (read: unemployed) scholars like myself wouldn't have to borrow "dependent" (read: employed) scholars' logins to their libraries?

I received a condescending and aggressive response from a woman who nevertheless went on to make some good points. "If you think that there aren't (. . .) non-scholars, who want to read articles in JSTOR or other online databases, you're living in a different world." The person in question made a series of good points: for the people writing Wikipedia pages, they need to have access to the "facts" so they aren't "spreading misinformation." And readers of Wikipedia need to be able to fact-check these assertions. More broadly, she went on, the debate has to do with "class, money, and elitism. Lack of information and lack of education are inextricably related problems not only in impoverished communities but in middle-class communities as well (even as that category shrinks in number)."

> Public libraries, public school students, home-schooling parents, freelancers (whether writing-related or in other fields), social justice activists . . . the list is endless. These are all groups that would benefit from being able to access scholarly articles with the latest developments, especially since there's so much misinformation being spread by public officials right now.

I thanked my friend's friend for her thought-provoking response, but asked if she wasn't overestimating the general interest in scholarship as well as the readability of much of those scholarly articles. My question wasn't about whether these articles *should* be readily available—which, why not, yes, let's do it—but why someone who wasn't a professional researcher, bound by the codes of the discipline to perform rigorous literature reviews and remain up-to-date with the latest research in their fields—would *want* to read them. She didn't reply. Open access is an important principle, worth fighting for, but what are we making available? The writing itself has to develop as well as the technology.

Some of the interesting work taking place at the intersection of academic and extra-academic inquiry goes by the name of para-academic writing, which Eileen Joy defines as capturing "the multivalent sense of something that fulfills and/or frustrates the academic from a position of intimate exteriority."

> Para-academia is that which is beside academia, a place whose logic encompasses many reasons and no reason at all (para-, "alongside, beyond, altered, contrary," from Greek para-, "beside, near, from, against, contrary to," cognate with Sanskrit para "beyond"). The para is the domain of: shadow, paradigm, daemon, parasite, supplement, amateur, elite.

I'd even include one of the most critically-acclaimed and best-selling books published in the US in 2015, Maggie Nelson's *The Argonauts*, under the heading of "para-academic." A hybrid work of memoir and criticism that addressed the author's queer family, gender, trans identity, and language, *The Argonauts* works its way through engagements with Roland Barthes, D.W. Winnicott, Eve Kosofsky Sedgwick, and Judith Butler: a list of names you'd be more likely to see in the bibliography of an academic monograph. Part of the reason Nelson's book took off as it did was thanks to the numerous reviews, interviews, and essays that were passed around online, on Twitter and Facebook; a search for "Maggie Nelson" on Tumblr turns up an endless number of quotations, and photographs of underlined books. The Internet is where we come together to share our enthusiasms, and careers are made there. And so a challenging book about gender, using weighty theoretical concepts, found its audience.

According to the editors of *The Para-Academic Handbook*, para-academics "mimic academic practices so they are liberated from the confines of the university," attempting to create "alternative, genuinely open access, learning-thinking-making-acting spaces on the Internet, in publications, in exhibitions, discussion groups or other mediums that seem appropriate to the situation." These include academic journals like *Continent*, or *Reconstruction: studies in contemporary culture* (on whose editorial board I serve) which do their own hosting and are freely available online. It often falls to individual writers and scholars to make the choice to make their work publicly available, whether this means writing for one of these open-access journals, or for the *Paris Review Daily*. Numerous online journals and magazines, like the *Los Angeles Review of Books*, *Public Books*, or *The New Inquiry* have opened up to fill this need. But we must go further to widen the field at both ends.

On his personal blog, the psychoanalyst Duane Rousselle warned against compromising the idea of para-academia, subsuming it back into the neoliberal university structures it was meant to attack. "[T]he goal was to infect the university with small bits of radical thinking. As a practice it encouraged radical students and professors to open up some space for thinking outside of the university so as to ensure that the university discourse did not get the final word over their desires."

Kristof complained that "[t]he latest attempt by academia to wall itself off from the world came when the executive council of the prestigious International Studies Association proposed that its publication editors be barred from having personal blogs. The association might as well scream: We want our scholars to be less influential!" But we're not walling ourselves off from the world; we're trying to find a way to talk to each other and to the world at large, and still make a living. Free-ranging, genre-defying criticism thrives on the Internet—in the websites and online magazines, in the blogs and the journals. Wherever inquiry is widely accessible, the digital critic can be a public critic. It's interesting that Kristof's op-ed appeared in the pages of the Sunday Book Review, suggesting that literary criticism is no less divorced from those "great debates," suggesting that such book review pages, and their online equivalents, can be the site of a necessary discussion about the way we live and why. Criticism wants to go outward.

A Media Of One's Own: The Future of Criticism, in Retrospect

Robert Barry

On the afternoon of January 19th, 2015, I was in a pub in North London to interview Thurston Moore. "The thing we established in punk rock is to *have your own media*," the former Sonic Youth guitarist reminisced over a mug of milky tea. "You *have your own media* now." A clear foot taller than me, Moore was laconic and assertive as he spoke. But a little later, on my way home, I started to wonder what he really meant by that statement, and to what degree it was really true. What is this media of our own?

He was referring, of course, to the Internet. Or, more specifically, to the particular paradigm of Internet culture that has been gathered under the questionable rubric of Web 2.0. Since the coining of the truncated neologisms "blog," "blogger," and "blogging" at the very end of the 1990s, the net has become host to an expanding number of sites whose aim is less to provide static pages for users to consume, and more to allow those users to actively intervene in adding music, video, opinion, and information of their own. All of a sudden, the web started to seem less like a settled text and more like a flexible, indeterminate "open work" in which everyone was invited to have their say.

In their opening address to the first Web 2.0 conference in San Francisco's Hotel Nikko in October 2004, publishers John Battelle and Tim O'Reilly introduced the notion of "the web as platform," referring to the dramatic growth in blogs hosted online and "adult Internet users who have contributed content to the Internet." These developments, they claimed, collectively provided the foundations of an "architecture of participation." Amazon, Napster, and eBay were all based on systems that relied on the input of ordinary users in order to take shape.

Thurston Moore is far from alone in seeing such structures as a new kind of media possessed by the people. When *Time* magazine nominated "you" as their "Person of the Year" two years after Battelle and O'Reilly addressed the Nikko Ballroom, the cover story cited "the cosmic compendium of knowledge Wikipedia and the million-channel people's network YouTube and the online metropolis MySpace" by way of justification. *Time* used its annual selection of an influential figure to fete the ordinary folks at home (like you!) for "seizing the reins of the global media." We were in charge now—or so the story went.

For Jeff Jarvis, Web 2.0 has been a source of consumer empowerment. In 2005, the American journalist bought a new computer. Pretty soon it ran into problems. Dissatisfied with the customer service he was experiencing, Jarvis took to his blog, Buzzmachine, and wrote a post with the title "Dell Sucks, Dell Lies." The title, he later insisted, was "not quite as juvenile as it sounds." Searching for any brand name followed by the word "sucks," Jarvis claimed, would invariably throw up what he called "the Consumer Reports of the people."

His blog post soon gathered steam. Before long, several thousand people had linked to it, commented on it, and added their stories, spreading it along to thousands more like them. Eventually, it even came to the attention of Dell themselves. The company finally relented and stumped up for a refund.

By this point, Jarvis was evidently coming to see himself rather like some eighteenth-century pamphleteer, a man with his "own printing press," as he declared in an article for *The Guardian*. In a later essay he went further. "Today," he wrote, "everyone has a press." But to what extent is Jarvis's "press" really his own?

Like many people of my generation, I used to have a MySpace page. You could do quite a lot with a MySpace page circa 2003. The early social networking site allowed you to add songs and videos to the page that bore your name. You could even customize it with HTML tags, changing its color and moving the page elements around. You could really make it your own. I remember thinking of it, rather proprietorially, as "my" page.

But then in July 2005, Rupert Murdoch's News Corporation bought MySpace for $580 million. Keen to make good on their investment, the new Murdoch-owned MySpace crammed its pages with more and more ads. I remember noticing that I wasn't getting a cut from the revenue accrued by the ads on "my" page. Due to the facility of customizing them, MySpace pages had always been somewhat colorful. Increasingly overburdened with ads, they began to look decidedly cluttered. Pages would take ages to load up. It got buggy. And then Facebook turned up, looking all smooth and smart.

In April 2008, Facebook overtook MySpace in popularity, plunging the latter into an irreversible decline. In 2011, the older site was formally put to bed. "My" page disappeared from the net with all the others. Turned out it had never really been mine to begin with.

In the years since then very little has changed, as Instagram users discovered in 2012 when that service was acquired by Facebook and they were promptly issued with new terms and conditions seemingly giving the company the right to exploit all their images without limit. Outside the walled gardens of social media, the situation is ultimately little different, albeit more complex. The lines of ownership and control are more obscure.

In the early days of the web, it was quite common for people to host their own websites on the hard drive of a domestic desktop. Today, for reasons of speed of loading, ease of access, or simply the impalpable allure of the cloud, it is more likely that the elements that comprise, say, Jeff Jarvis's Buzzmachine blog will find their material existence distributed across multiple servers in anonymous-looking data centers in Las Vegas, Langfang, and Bluffdale, Utah. None of which are really owned by Jarvis himself—not in the way that a radio station might own its studio, transmission lines, and antenna.

Even the digital door keys that link the memorable phrase "buzz-machine" to a string of numbers in machine code that tell your computer how to find the page in question are no more than leased by Jarvis from a third party domain name registrar. In the event of their sudden bankruptcy, the blog would be lost, even to Jarvis himself. So to say that he has his own press—that we *all* now have our printing presses—is pushing it, to say the least.

To speak of having a press, of having a media of one's own, suggests infrastructure. But the question of infrastructure is curiously absent from panegyrics to the liberating force of the net. Jeff Jarvis doesn't mention million dollar undersea cables, as thick as a Coke can and a hundred thousand miles long, coated with galvanized shielding wire. When *Time* nominated you person of the year, they neglected to touch upon space frame warehouses of a million square feet, stuffed to the gills with servers that eat daily the same energy as a small town.

By their own estimates, Google is one of the world's biggest hardware manufacturers. But none of the computers they build is for sale. They are made to stock the company's many data centers in Finland, Chile, Belgium, and Taiwan. Just one of their facilities in Wasco County, Oregon, can boast forty-five shipping containers with over a thousand servers each.

All of which seems commonly to evanesce into metaphors of clouds, streams, and cosmic nebulae. Look a little closer at the promise of *our* media and it quickly dissipates into the fiction of *no media at all*. Just a few months before I met Thurston Moore I had been struck by a line in a keynote speech from his contemporary on the American alternative rock scene, Steve Albini. Addressing a music industry conference in Melbourne, the famously prickly producer of Nirvana and the Pixies praised the Internet for allowing audiences to "develop direct relationships" with artists. *Time's* cover story, likewise, spoke of new forms of communication "citizen to citizen, person to person" as if there were nothing between the two. For Jeff Jarvis, Google is a "post-media company," a phrase that suggests the distortions of twentieth-century communications technologies have all been overcome, that all intermediaries are now redundant (or will be soon).

This coinage is not quite original to Jarvis. In the late 80s, the French philosopher-psychotherapist Félix Guattari was already trumping up the transition from "the mass-media era to a *post-media* age, in which the media will be reappropriated by a multitude of subject-groups capable of directing its resingularization." But Guattari had never even heard of the Internet. He would be dead before the release of the first popular web browser. When he spoke of "post-media" he had been stirred, mostly, by a technology called Minitel, a simple French videotex service that allowed passengers at rail stations to buy concert tickets and check stock prices from public terminals. Its most common use was as a screen-based telephone directory.

But if Guattari's fervor for a system whose revolutionary interactivity scarcely exceeded that of a game of Pong seems surprising, listen to the voices of today's dot com enthusiasts. "We don't need the gatekeepers anymore," said Courtney Love, another voice from the alternative rock scene, to a conference in New York in the spring of 2000. I've been quoting a lot of music industry figures in this essay because, thanks to development of file-sharing sites like Napster and the convenience and compactness of the mp3 format, a lot of the changes that the Internet is bringing about in other fields happened first—and hit hardest—in music. When Love talks about gatekeepers, she's talking quite specifically about record labels, artist managers, concert promoters, and radio producers. But increasingly this quasi-mythical figure of the "gatekeeper" has entered the discourse of the publishing trade. "Today, you can bypass the gatekeepers," claimed Andy Weir, the author whose self-published novel *The Martian* became a Hollywood film starring Matt Damon, in a podcast interview with author and hedge fund manager James Altucher.

Like the god Telipinu, the mediatic gatekeeper is a figure evoked only to announce its disappearance. Unlike the Hittite farmer deity, though, this gatekeeper's disappearance apparently brings only abundance. Our communications are now "direct," unfiltered, untrammeled. Our artists produce and connect with their audiences without restraint or intercession. Like the "ether" of Victorian spiritualists, the net promises a fantasy of perfect communion, a medium that does not mediate.

But what of the Internet service providers, web hosting providers, domain name registrars, search engines and search engine optimization companies, recommendation algorithms, ad servers, content discovery platforms, online identity managers, and social networks? Upon closer analysis, the web quickly turns out to have produced an overwhelming profusion of new kinds of gatekeepers. These new intermediaries appear perfectly inert and transparent— until you try posting a nipple on Facebook or searching for free mp3s on a Virgin Media connection. The immediacy of new media may be their greatest ideological trick.

Despite this, the web has undoubtedly produced a certain feeling of empowerment for many of its users, the tangible effects of which should not be dismissed lightly. Think of Jeff Jarvis and his "Consumer Reports of the people." Here, perhaps, is criticism in its rawest form. The capacity to say, this sucks, and have others pay heed. "On the Internet," the *New York Times* recently declared, "everyone is a critic."

In 1997, James Berardinelli—the subject of an *L.A. Times*'s article entitled "In Online World, Everyone Can Be A Critic"—had to actively choose to start his ReelViews film review website. Today, we can scarcely get in a cab, buy a toaster, or use a public convenience without having our opinion of the experience demanded of us by some web-enabled device or other.

This development was already somewhat anticipated by the critic Armond White's 1989 suggestion that "in the future, everyone will be film critics"—a statement almost perfectly reproduced (while given new resonance in the social media age) in a post on Twitter by another critic, Ryan McGee, on the ninth of July, 2015. "In the future," he wrote, "everyone will be an online TV/film critic for fifteen minutes each night after their actual bill-paying job." If this is beginning to sound like a Philip K. Dick novel, surely one of the oddest things about McGee's tweet is that he continues to project into the future what, as a Twitter user, he must already be witnessing on a nightly basis.

I shan't, for the time being at least, be wringing my professional critic's hands over what this means for the sanctity and security of my job. I merely question to what extent this is a phenomenon strictly limited to the present. Thurston Moore had already spoken of the attempts to establish samizdat forms of media in the punk era of late 70s New York. Arriving in the city in 1976, Moore would have encountered a blossoming profusion of unofficial communication channels in the form of flyers, posters, and fanzines, cheaply photocopied, wallpapering the downtown streets or handed out at gigs. Xerography, that seemingly most bureaucratic of inventions, became what Kate Eichhorn has called "the Trojan horse of the punk movement."

As Eichhorn argues in her recent book *Adjusted Margin*, photocopying provided the perfect technology for leftfield artists and activists in the 70s and 80s due to the easy availability of low-cost copy shops, the perfect anonymity of such institutions, and the lack of any trace or master copy left by the reproduction process in the machine itself. In contradistinction to the net (after the revelations of Edward Snowden), nobody at the copy shop knows you are a dog. At least, no post-facto metadata analysis could prove it. Photocopying was cheap, fast, and—for a while—close to ubiquitous. By the time Courtney Love formed her band, Hole, in 1989, there was a remarkably resilient network of 'zine producers around the world, exchanging their wares by mail, at gigs, and through independent record stores.

Though you might search for antecedents in the amateur press associations of the late nineteenth and early twentieth centuries (of which a young H.P. Lovecraft was a member), the origins of the fanzine movement inherited by punk lie in the cloistered world of science fiction fandom. The very term "science fiction" was invented by a Luxembourgian expat in New York named Hugo Gernsback. An inventor and entrepreneur by trade, he arrived at the publishing industry from a background selling radio parts to hobbyists. His first magazines were little more than catalogs that only gradually introduced more and more editorial content.

With his *Amazing Stories*, from April 1926, he produced the very first regular journal devoted to the field he first dubbed "scientifiction." Evidently quite unprepared for the flood of enthusiasm for his new publication, Gernsback soon found himself inundated with appreciative letters from his readers. From January 1927, he began to publish these letters in a new "Discussions" column in the magazine itself, playing host to sometimes lengthy debates on the merits and scientific plausibility of the stories he printed. From the beginning of the following year, he began to print not just the letter with the correspondent's name and home town, but also their actual home address. This may seem like a small step, but its effect was profound. It allowed the readers to correspond with each other by mail, independent of Gernsback's editorial eye.

Almost immediately, the first scientifiction fanclubs started emerging, actively encouraged by Gernsback himself in the pages of his magazine. As Aubrey MacDermott, founder of one of the earliest such groups, recalled in a letter to fanzine writer Andy Porter in 1990, upon picking up the new *Amazing Stories* in the spring of 1928, he discovered "Gernsback had something new. He printed names and addresses of correspondents. I had for years been writing to authors and now I could write to fans. When I returned to East Oakland in April 1928, the first thing I did was to contact fans, Clifton Amsbury in Berkeley, Louis Smith in East Oakland, and Lester Anderson in Hayward. That was the start of our fan club."

Another prominent early group was known as the Science Correspondents Club. It was this group that in 1930 began producing *The Comet*, probably the first science fiction fanzine. Even though the hand-drawn, mimeographed pages of *The Comet* were filled mostly with articles about science and extended debate about the stories in *Amazing Stories* that couldn't be contained in "Discussions," it would nonetheless produce many imitators with far more varied contents. In his memoirs, the prominent science fiction author Frederick Pohl recalls his own youthful days as a reader/writer of fanzines (in practice the distinction tended to be fragile): "The best article I have ever read on hand-to-hand combat in space was written by Harry Harrison and published in the fanzine *Amra*. All that I know about mescaline comes from a fanzine article by Bill Donaho. Damon Knight made his original reputation as a science-fiction critic by a surgical dissection of the quivering flesh of A.E. van Vogt, in a fanzine article when van Vogt was at the height of his popularity."

At times, Pohl admits, the content of the zines he edited and collected was "not very good at all." But at their best (and sometimes at their worst), the fanzines produced a form of literature that is hard to imagine developing in their absence. The zines Pohl worked on published clubhouse news, fiction reviews, "gossip," letters, stories, and poems. "Sometimes," he notes, "they were a kind of writing for which professional markets did not seem to exist." The Harry Harrison piece mentioned above sounds almost like an entirely new genre of speculative criticism, in which the generic tropes of fact and fiction freely intermingle.

There was a radical openness to fanzine production that was clearly the source both of the genre's triumphs and its embarrassments, "because," Pohl explains, "there are no standards of excellence that fanzines must meet. Not *any*. All it takes to publish a fanzine is the will to make it happen, and maybe access to somebody else's mimeograph machine, and in a pinch you can get by without the latter." For perhaps the first time, anyone could be a critic. Amongst stories of space exploration and utopian tomorrows, the future of criticism found its origin in a rush of futurist speculation.

There was nothing transparent about mimeograph and xerography as media. Many zines did little else but talk about zine production. Meta-zines like *Factsheet 5* reported on other zines. Few accounts of the fanzine history pass without some mention of smudged fingers and low-resolution imagery. The production process was evident all over every product. The peculiar grain of photocopied pages became the object of artistic practice. Ian Burn, for instance, in 1968, produced his *Xerox Book* by placing a blank sheet of paper under the hood of a Xerox 720 machine and pressing "copy." As the xerographic reproduction issued from the machine's rollers and into the out tray, he replaced the original white sheet under the lid with the copy he made. Again he pressed copy, and again, going on to repeat this process until he was left with a volume of 100 pages showing a gradually deteriorating clear surface, steadily being overcome by the artifacts of the reproduction process until the last few pages were completely black. The distinction between production and reproduction collapsed in a flash of light and a whir of inked rollers.

Was this a media of our own? Not really. Kinko's still owned the means of production. But access—if not quite convenience—was about as open as it is online. What finally separates the everyman critics of the ink-stained era from the bloggers of the twenty-first century is finally a question of context. On the Internet, that context is almost inevitably one framed and supported by advertising. Social media—and in this respect that includes Google—offer their users free services in exchange for data which is harvested and processed in order to sell those audiences to advertisers. The kind of behaviors encouraged by such a system would tend to be those which reinforce the user's status as shopper. Search "reviews" on Google and the first thing that comes up is TripAdvisor.

For now, criticism as a compulsory activity carried out by all people equally is inextricable from the circuits of consumption and exchange. Online, everyone is a critic—but only insofar as everyone is also a consumer.

Book Lovers: Literary Necrophilia in the 21st Century

Joanna Walsh

Recently I was emailing with a friend about the new book by Geoff Dyer and I said: "Is that piece he wrote for the *LRB* about having a stroke in it? My take-home from that was a deep envy of the 'twice-baked hazelnut croissants' he ate every day in LA. Come to think of it, I remember a croissant in the piece he wrote for *Yoga* too. I think it was almond. Maybe he really likes croissants." A few emails before, my friend was telling me an anecdote about the French author, Michel Houellebecq, who is a regular visitor to a bar where his friend works. We speculated about Houellebecq's tastes as evinced in his writing—which, like Dyer's, is often autofictional—for "fancy French reds." We wanted to know more about Houellebecq, about Dyer, and we combed their texts for clues, as though knowing were the point. Reading this way made us feel cool. It also made us feel a bit fake.

In 1967 the French theorist, Roland Barthes, said the author was dead, shifting the burden of textual meaning to the reader. "To give the text an author," he wrote, "is to impose a limit on the text." In *What Is An Author* (1969), often considered a response to Barthes' work, the French theorist, Michel Foucault wrote: "The author is therefore the ideological figure by which one marks the manner in which we fear the proliferation of meaning." It was around that time that my parents, who loved books, bought vast numbers of cheap paperbacks, which were cheaper than they ever had been. My parents rarely saw even a jacket photo of these books' authors who, until they died and their biographies were written, gave little or no account of their lives outside what could be deduced from within the limits of the texts they produced. Just as the idea of the author provided limits for the textual meaning, the texts provided limits within which these limiting author-figures could be constructed.

In 1967, it really was possible to be a "book lover." What readers loved about books was sometimes the language, the story, but this very seldom occurred without their also loving the characters. To love a character could be, to paraphrase Barthes, *a way of putting a limit on love*. Characters could also be, after Foucault, *the ideological figures by which one marks the manner in which we fear love's proliferation*. This love was accompanied by the anxiety of their knowledge that these people were fake.

In 2007 the author Sheila Heti wrote, of her autofiction *How Should a Person Be?*: "Increasingly I'm less interested in writing about fictional people, because it seems so tiresome to make up a fake persona and put them through the paces of a fake story. I just—I can't do it." The line between "fiction" and autobiography from the twentieth and into the twenty-first century has acted as an increasingly sharply-acknowledged focus for anxiety grouped around ideas of fakeness, and consequently of authenticity, and so of "virtue" in terms of moral good and quality of writing. But it is "fake" writing—the ability and intention to make up a "persona"—that has historically been seen as "good" writing. Autobiographical writing in fiction has been decried as "bad" writing, and an admission of autobiography as what identifies a "fake" writer.

The philosopher Martin Heidegger thought autobiography had nothing to do with "good" writing. Of Aristotle he said "He was born, he thought, he died. And all the rest is pure anecdote." I cannot track down this quote to identify it with its speaker, as the story is itself anecdotal. It was told by Jacques Derrida in the film, *Derrida* (2002), a purely anecdotal biography that shows the French philosopher making some breakfast that is not a croissant, and choosing his teaching suits, but little of his work, other than what is revealed through his everyday activities. Jacques Derrida, author of *Circumfession*, an autobiography written in collaboration ("this book presupposes a contract") with the scholar Geoffrey Bennington, and published in their jointly-written book, *Jacques Derrida* (1999), valued autobiography in a writer's work. In the biographical film, *Derrida*, he asked "Why have [philosophers] effaced their private lives in their work? Why do they never talk about personal things? I'm not saying someone should make a porn film about Hegel or Heidegger. I want to hear them talking about the part love plays in their lives."

In 2012 Sheila Heti responded to critics who panned her book for directly discussing the part love (both friendly and erotic) plays in her life: "People who look at themselves in order to better look at the world—that is not narcissism. It is, and has always been, what people who make art do, and must do. You cannot do it blind. You cannot do it by looking at a toaster." Heti implicitly accepts her critics' point that "narcissistic writing"—presumably writing that demands and relies on a legitimizing response from the reader—is both morally undesirable and equivalent to "bad" writing. In 1947 Truman Capote published *Other Voices, Other Rooms*, a novel he only later recognized as autobiographical. "Rereading it now," he said later in 1972, as related in an anecdote written by Gerald Clarke in his biography *Capote* (2013), "I find such self-deception unpardonable." The autobiographical material about the part love played in Truman Capote's life in *Other Voices, Other Rooms* was hidden in fiction and the author escaped accusations of "narcissism" exactly because his material was considered "immoral" enough for him to—by fictionalizing it—practice a deception on himself and, by extension, his reader. That the fictional and the immoral are close companions can be revealed only when fiction is "narcissistically" confessed to be autobiographical, at which point its writer encounters the double bind of having written not only "immorally" but "badly."

While the potentially controversial autobiographical subject matter of *Other Voices, Other Rooms* went under the radar, Truman Capote's "seductive" author photo appearing, unusually for the time, on the book's jacket made him instantly recognizable, and caused, wrote his biographer, Gerald Clarke, "uproar… He had not foreseen that the picture would overshadow, and in some ways trivialize, the work it was promoting, transforming the real right thing into something that many dismissed as the product of a brilliant publicity campaign." Clarke relates how Random House's publicity posters for the book showed the photograph, with the strapline: "This is Truman Capote."

Capote's image became his acknowledged avatar, a communiqué from the author that bypassed his work. Another Clarke anecdote goes that, while Capote denied complicity with the campaign in public, he colluded with it enthusiastically in private. In *The Words of Selves* (2000) Denise Riley wrote: "My self-definition can be a determined appeal for recognition… In some sense it may well be performative, like a first declaration of love." Wikipedia puts the date of the "Affective Turn"—the rise of the study of affective theory and emotion in the humanities and sciences—also in the year 2000. In 2015 the star of approval on Twitter turned into the heart of affection. We are no longer giving prizes for writing: what we are giving is (and is for) something else.

I think my metaphor is *falling in love*. Wait, I didn't mean metaphor, I meant metier: some kind of work. Of art.

❖   ❖   ❖

In 2016, I talked to the American poet Anne Boyer about the regular "suiciding" of her Twitter account. She had, she said, become *addicted to self-destruction.* She also spoke of the labor of *accounting for yourself* in writing. In *Wages Against Housework* (1975), Silvia Federici says: "Many times the difficulties and ambiguities which women express in discussing wages for housework stem from the reduction of wages for housework to a thing, a lump of money, instead of viewing it as a political perspective. The difference between these two standpoints is enormous. To view wages for housework as a thing rather than a perspective is to detach the end result of our struggle from the struggle itself." Or she could have said "Many times the difficulties and ambiguities which authors express in discussing wages for *accounting for yourself* stem from the reduction of wages for *accounting for yourself* to an object, a lump of money, instead of viewing it as a political perspective. The difference between these two standpoints is enormous. To view wages for *accounting for yourself* as an object rather than a perspective is to detach the end result of our struggle from the struggle itself."

In 2016 an author undertakes the labor of *self-accounting* online. Of course it is possible to avoid self-accounting, just as it would have been possible for Capote, in 1947, to have written a novel that gave an open account of him life, but the demands of contemporary culture weigh against both. On social media authors fake themselves, drawing up accounts of themselves as digital objects, differently from the ways an author-figure can be constructed via the pages of a book. Dyer's croissants made me and my friend feel cool as readers not only, perhaps, in the sense of being post-morally disengaged from the affective possibilities of the text (its characters, its language) but also in the McLuhanian sense, drawn into a critical game of constructing the author from a series of associated objects across different media, in this case crucially beyond the limits of the text. The game (as Federici says, the "perspective") seemed the point.

An object in digital programming is not, as Federici puts it "a lump": it works a bit more like an anecdote. It is a set of data, plus a method. A programmed object is its characteristics, plus how it is used: its data is encapsulated in its functions. Why call it an object at all, why fit it to a figure of speech? Well, programming is semantic. Names are grasping tools, bridging the gap between concept and code, and what they grasp is physical, or so it appears. The language of programming is one of metaphor: its "objects" correspond to things found in the real world. When we think of data + method as a "library," or a "checkout," it's easier to understand, to maintain, to evolve the virtual, but this also means our behaviors are carried over from the meatspace. A programming "object" is a real white elephant in the room, a whatnot, a bibelot, a conversation piece: useless in itself until it demands our response. Its metaphors are social, familial, the stuff of private lives, or anecdote (as in the real world, "inheritance" give rise to a "hierarchy"—behaviors are carried across from one object to all its "relations"). Textual meaning is best located in the author-space into which can be put any number of possible anecdotes (aka digital objects) hinging on seemingly 3D anecdotal objects such as croissants, teaching suits, and *fancy French reds*. The burden of fakeness shifts to the reader. Now it is as possible to fall in love with a croissant as a book. And I mean the word "croissant."

(In the meantime, I would like to read a novel about a toaster.)

The Italian writer Elena Ferrante does not have an author photo. This is not the same as not having an author photo in 1947, or in 1967. It is her lack of photo that now invites anecdote. To have a biography means you must not *account for yourself.*

"The anecdote," said the poet Anne Boyer, when I met her for the first time in the flesh and not on Twitter, in 2016, "resists authority." Until late 2016 there were no anecdotes about Elena Ferrante, only about readers' experiences of *accounting for* Elena Ferrante, including guesses as to her age, sex, nationality, inheritance, hierarchy, and familial and professional relations. Ferrrante was not a "dead" author as she had no public identity from which to "suicide" (the only contemporary option open), and so provided readers with no limit, no ability to mark their fear of love's proliferation. Given few other objects to work with, readers often tried to identify her by traditional means, via her books, and the accounts she gave, in them, of her characters' lives. This labor, shifted to the reader, is not in an *appeal for recognition* by the writer, but marks a corresponding desire, in the reader, to recognize. With books no longer a reliable holding zone for implicit autobiography, Ferrante's refusal either to admit or hide her "narcissism" shifted the moral burden of creating meaning back to her readers who, once more, were left to attempt to mark their anxiety via the limits of their creation.

"They say it is love," wrote Silvia Federici in *Wages Against Housework*. "We say it is unwaged work."

Topical Criticism and the Cultural Logic of the Quick Take

Louis Bury

It wouldn't be too much of a stretch to flatter ourselves that we live in a golden era of literary criticism. The Internet has not only extended the popular reach of book culture, in venues as different as *The Millions* and *BuzzFeed*, but it has also, in venues such as *n+1* and *The Los Angeles Review of Books*, granted academics permission to write for audiences of non-specialists in salutary and discerning ways. What's more, literary criticism now takes increasingly varied and daring forms. Thanks to pioneers of experimental criticism such as Chris Kraus, Geoff Dyer, and Wayne Koestenbaum, lively book-length critical excursions that either invent or dissolve a genre have in recent years become a genre unto themselves. In short, as literary criticism has enjoyed greater circulation and relevance, it has also, in the hands of writers such as Maggie Nelson and Claudia Rankine, come to encompass some of the most urgent and ambitious writing around today. Critics, beleaguered handmaidens of the arts, could be forgiven for imagining that their station has risen of late.

But for all of literary criticism's increased visibility and élan, digital culture has also caused it to develop any number of counterproductive habits. The list of its vices is as predictable as it is irritating: the proliferation of vacuous think pieces; the race for immediacy of response; the endless patter of Twitter, Facebook, and Goodreads; the clickbait headlines; the indignant witch hunts and sensationalist bonfires; the nutritionless listicles. Certain individual critics do seem the deserved recipients of great esteem but critics as a species still get regarded, as ever, like sports officials: taken for granted when they perform their job well, scorned when they misstep.

Many of these less desirable critical tendencies converge today, like never before, in the form of topical criticism. As I use it here, topical criticism refers to critical takes that respond to breaking, of-the-moment, often scandalous or sensational news, the kind of news that, once discovered, spreads across literary Twitter like small-town gossip. Topical criticism has always existed in one form or another but it has newly distinguished itself as the characteristic, if hitherto unnamed, form of criticism in the digital age, the form that most embodies a prominent strain of values in online critical practice today. In its eminent shareability, topical criticism constitutes the form according to which practitioners imagine what it means to be heard—to be influential—as a critic. It is the form par excellence of putting one's foot down in cyberspace.

More even than its veneer of authority, topical criticism's animating feature is its timeliness. As in our networked personal lives, the expected response time in online critical discourse has accelerated to the point where the appearance of hair-trigger critical "takes" seems normal, even desirable. The critical take's contents and publication venue still matters to its reception, as does its author's expertise and reputation, but the rapidity with which it appears has increasingly come to define the form. The form's ideal, whether individual critics aspire to it or not, consists in getting shared widely enough, fast enough, so as to become the *de facto* authoritative take, the one that sets the terms of debate for the many other takes and counter-takes to follow. The scramble to pen the first viral take constitutes the rough analog, albeit with a stark difference in tone, of writing "first!" in the comments section of a popular blog, in that both of these gestures mark off territory to indicate an author's priority, mocking or serious, in the anticipated discourse.

This accelerated rate of response occurs throughout digital culture and is by no means a phenomenon particular to the rarefied realm of literary criticism. But its existence—its pervasiveness—even in high literary contexts should alert us to just how dramatically the Internet has adjusted expectations for the time horizon of critical thought. Even before it was considered quaint and old-fashioned, as a hapless turtle on the shoulder of the information superhighway, literature has always been the cultural activity most conducive to slow, considered thought. It is not just that reading and writing take time to perform but that they are activities well-suited to mulling over issues that don't yield to immediate understanding. Even when born out of deep knowledge and experience, snap reactions and speed screeds run counter to the spirit and nature of the literary enterprise. Literature prefers—or at least used to prefer—its ideas better digested.

In what follows, I survey digitally published responses to two prominent poetry controversies that occurred in 2015, a year pocked with literary scandal in the United States. My account focuses on the initial responses to conceptual poet Kenneth Goldsmith's performance of "The Body of Michael Brown," but does not weigh in on the debates in any substantial way. Instead, I consider these two related flurries of critical activity, reactions to scandals occasioned by Goldsmith and his fellow Conceptualist Vanessa Place, as case studies in the cultural logic of responsiveness. Poetry may indeed be news that stays news, as Ezra Pound had it, but recent poetry imbroglios have not always been quite so lasting, and have instead, with important exceptions, followed the general news cycle's pattern of headlong response and then headlong indifference.

However, rather than simply evidencing a decline in considered critical thought, recent poetry controversies also illustrate how cycles of digital response can speed up the process of consensus-building disputation that has always, from the pages of Addison and Steele's *The Spectator* to the open-air debates of the Greek agora, been the Zenonian endpoint towards which critical discourse tries to refine itself. Even as the online argumentation of the most hurried individual critics tends to become sloppier and better visible, the argumentation of the collective critical whole tends to refine itself faster. In this light, the perceived cultural imperative to be responsive, posthaste, derives not, as would be expected, from a social pressure to remain connected and in touch at all times, but, rather, in ways at once beneficent and frightening, from an epistemological pressure not to dwell in "unknowing" one moment longer than necessary.

On March 13, 2015, as part of Brown University's Interrupt 3 conference, prominent American poet Kenneth Goldsmith performed a controversial poem called "The Body of Michael Brown," a poem which even his apologists acknowledge was hurtful and ill-advised. The poem consisted of a slightly altered transcription of the autopsy report of Michael Brown, the African-American teenager shot and killed on August 9, 2014 by Darren Wilson, a white police officer in Ferguson, Missouri. Brown's killing, and the ensuing trial, sparked nationwide protests and galvanized the emerging Black Lives Matter movement.

At the time of the performance, Goldsmith had already achieved considerable notoriety—a 2011 poetry reading at the White House; a 2013 appearance on the Colbert Report; the 2013 title of MoMA's inaugural Poet Laureate. He had become the figurehead of Conceptual Poetry, an early 21st-century literary movement best known for bringing Marcel Duchamp's appropriative artistic practice to the literary and digital realms. As a species of artistic transcription, "The Body of Michael Brown" was thus of a piece with Goldsmith's previous poetic output, especially his 2013 *Seven American Deaths and Disasters*, a collection of lightly edited radio and television transcripts of public catastrophes such as John F. Kennedy's assassination and the World Trade Center attacks of September 11th.

But unlike the edits made to the transcripts in *Seven American Deaths*, such as the decisions to include or exclude commercials, the edits made to "The Body of Michael Brown" were injudicious and telling. In particular, Goldsmith's cheap and sensational decision to end the thirty-minute performance with the coroner's description of Brown's genitals as "unremarkable" participates in a long line of baleful stereotypes that eroticize and objectify black men on the basis of their genitalia. Even apart from the poem's ending, many commentators took issue with the way the performance's conceit utilized a black man's body for a white man's personal gain, another racist pattern with a long and painful history in the United States.

Because Goldsmith requested that Brown University not release the video recording of his performance, on the grounds that he didn't want to cause any more undue anguish to Michael Brown's family and others, "The Body of Michael Brown" has never been seen or read by anyone other than the approximately seventy-five audience members in attendance at its lone performance. Instead, all information about the poem and its performance arrived to the general public second-hand via social media posts and audience members' published accounts.

This epistemological remove turns out to be less consequential than might be imagined. For one thing, almost all commentators who did not attend the performance caveat that they were not there to witness it and modulate their commentary accordingly. For another, one of the cornerstones of Goldsmith's esthetic philosophy has long been that "you really don't need to read [my works] to get the idea of what they're like; you just need to know the general concept," an all-too-fitting axiom for a performance whose conceit alone has been the greatest source of consternation in responses to it.

Still, it seems ironic and somehow apt that an unviewable performance should occasion so much digital commentary. Everybody in the poetry world found themselves talking and writing about a poem that almost nobody had seen or read. This state of affairs—commenting on something without having experienced it oneself—may have been necessary in this particular situation but is, in several ways, an all too common feature of digital discourse. Commentary, supposedly a secondary, parasitic form of discourse, can become, online, a primary form of discourse, an end unto itself, an activity that eclipses the thing being commented upon because it has surprisingly little to do with it. Even in circumstances where the primary source is better available for inspection than Goldsmith's performance, digital commentary can cover that source over, kudzu-like, until only its faint outline remains.

In the case of "The Body of Michael Brown," the performance's unavailability created not only a sprawling thicket of commentary but also an inadvertent archive of description and response, especially on social media. Looking back over that record, the timeline of responses illustrates how, day-by-day, formal commentary on the performance appeared with increasing velocity. It also points up the way in which digital criticism occurs over two distinct time horizons, one immediate and compact in duration, the other slower and more spread out across the calendar.

In capsule form, here is the 2015 timeline of responses to "The Body of Michael Brown." On Friday, March 13, the evening of Goldsmith's performance, a handful of live-tweets and post-event tweets appear. On Saturday, March 14, tweets about the performance increase in quantity, increase in the amount of attention they receive, and increase in the amount of anger towards Goldsmith they express. The first viral critical take, a blog post by the writer Jacqueline Valencia that responds to the information disclosed in the previous days' tweets, appears on Sunday, March 15. Over the next three days, as the workweek begins, an avalanche of critical takes appear, dozens of them, in outlets both major and obscure, cascading down social media feeds throughout the literary community. This publishing frenzy eases after Wednesday, March 18th, though a handful of more takes, increasingly synthetic in nature, still trickle in for another week or so. This initial burst of activity, an eclipse of moths descending upon the flame of scandal, takes place over seven to ten excitable days and comprises the first time horizon of critical response.

The second time horizon takes place over the next six to twelve months. In contrast to the first time period, where so many published takes, to say nothing of informal social media posts, appear in such a short time span that it becomes near impossible to keep up with them all, during this next time period it is silence, punctuated by retrospective takes, that becomes the defining mode of discourse. If the literary public hasn't forgotten about the event, exactly, it has at least relaxed its initial python squeeze. When new takes do appear they are usually occasioned by a related piece of breaking news, a pattern seen in the general news cycle, as when, in the past several years, the latest American episode of mass shooting or police brutality prompts reflections on other recent, but temporarily forgotten, such episodes.

The longer durée of responses to Goldsmith's performance fits this pattern. Within two weeks of the performance, substantial new critical takes on it effectively cease to appear until, in May of that same year, Goldsmith's fellow Conceptualist, Vanessa Place, attracts substantial criticism for a Twitter project in which she tweets out, verbatim, the racist text of Margaret Mitchell's 1936 novel *Gone With the Wind* and uses, as the account page's image, a stereotypical film still of the late black actress Hattie McDaniel as the character Mammy. After the Place controversy, focus on Goldsmith's performance again cools down until the *New Yorker* runs a sympathetic profile of him in October, which prompts another round of takes and reflections, especially regarding the article's depiction of the poet Cathy Park Hong, who felt the piece misrepresented her in unfair and telling ways. Finally, in November and December, several venues run year-end style meditations on race and literature that center around the Goldsmith and Place controversies: *Entropy Magazine* and *The Los Angeles Review of Books* each publish retrospective takes on the topic; *Boundary2*, a journal published by Duke University, dedicates an entire issue to a poetry-centric "Dossier" on "Race and Innovation." As a rule, these laggard takes tend to be synthetic in nature, consolidating the welter of positions taken earlier in the year so as to identify, with the benefit of hindsight, the key terms of debate and then move the conversation forward.

Even when recapitulated, as above, in synoptic, timeline form, the responses to Goldsmith's performance, to say nothing of the responses to Place's, are intricate and involved to describe. Like all criticism, they have something of a he-said, she-said quality to them. Their difference from the literary criticism of even a couple of decades ago, however, consists in the rapidity with which the arguments, counter-arguments, and recriminations get made. In aggregate, reading the initial onrush of critical takes can feel like watching a time-lapse film of a debate's evolution. Published ideas that used to take months, if not years, to filter through the sieves of multiple critics' minds can now undergo that process in a matter of weeks, if not days. To capture a more fine-grained sense of that process, I now turn my attention to the particulars of the argumentation made in response to Goldsmith's work.

The initial tweets in response to Goldsmith's performance range from neutral and descriptive (Paul Soulellis: "Kenneth Goldsmith reading a new work The Body of Michael Brown, the autopsy report") to mocking (OrlandoLuisPardoLazo: "Unlistening unto unpoet Kenneth Goldsmith") to outraged (jay santa cruz: "@kg_ubu you're a ghoul and a vulture. a fucking cannibal."). But the majority of the tweets from that weekend strike a tone of polemical dialog. "Pretty wild that as a white man you tout an esthetics of theft and apply that to a black body," tweeted Grant Bishop at Goldsmith, "you should just apologize!" "It's not that you do or don't have the right to do what you did," Kyla Wazana Tompkins rebuked Goldsmith, "It is that you do not feel responsible for the harm it inflicts." In tweets such as Bishop's and Wazana Tompkins', you can already see, in germinal form, the outlines of what would become some of the major lines of critique in the coming days.

One of the more sustained Twitter considerations of the performance came from the account of Braydon Beaulieu in the form of twelve numbered and ruminative reactions. Displaying a bit more tentativeness than would characterize responses in the days to follow, Beaulieu explained that "I was not at this reading, but tweets by those who were, suggest that Goldsmith's performance might not have been respectful," and argued that "regardless of the specifics of his performance, his appropriation of black suffering is inherently problematic." He then went on to provide links to already-published works on the topic of race and poetry: a February 2015 essay in *Entropy Magazine* by Michael Hessel-Mial called "Conceptual Writing in the Time of Non-Indictment"; a March 2015 feature in the *Boston Review* on "Race and the Poetic Avant-Garde."

Beaulieu's response to the performance stands out less for the content of its argumentation than for the way it makes apparent that a version of the critical conversation that is about to take place in the coming days has actually already been taking place. Poet and editor Stefania Heim's introduction to the *Boston Review* feature that Beaulieu cites, published on March 10, 2015, just three days before Goldsmith's performance, provides a sense of the many layers to this discursive onion. Heim situates recent critical conversations about race and avant-garde poetry, such as poet Cathy Park Hong's influential November 2014 *Lana Turner* essay "Delusions of Whiteness in the Avant-Garde," in the context of poet Harryette Mullen's "decades-old description" of the false assumption that African-American poetry is not "formally innovative."

Among the recent critical takes which Heim cites is poet and translator Daniel Borzutsky's December 2014 Poetry Foundation's *Harriet* blog response to Park Hong's essay, "Delusions of Progress," in which Borzutsky spells out in greater detail a latent element in Heim's rationale for the *Boston Review* feature. In a rambling but informative history lesson, Borzutsky shows how Park Hong's argument about the racism of Conceptual Poetry and other American poetic avant-gardes, while urgent and true, is in fact nothing new but an argument that, in one form or another, critics have been making for decades. Borzutsky speculates, compellingly, that part of why Park Hong's essay garnered so much attention is because it appeared during the autumn after Michael Brown's murder, a time in the United States when "the rage and resistance to the police murders of unarmed black men [was] so alive and visible." The timing was right for Park Hong's updated version of a decades-old argument to get noticed.

In other words, it takes the right set of outside circumstances, scandal especially, for an ongoing critical conversation—and all such conversations are ongoing—to obtain a critical mass of attention, a process that happens more easily in the digital era. In the case of the conversation about the racial politics of Conceptual esthetics, you can look back, with the benefit of hindsight, and see any number of critical takes that anticipate the fevered debates about Goldsmith's performance and Place's text. Borzutsky's essay alone identifies a syllabus' worth of recent antecedents: Sueyeun Juliette Lee's May 2014 *The Volta* essay "Shock and Blah: Offensive Postures in Conceptual Poetry and the Traumatic Stuplime"; Evie Shockley's 2013 *Jacket2* essay, "Is 'Zong!' Conceptual Poetry? Yes, it isn't"; Dorothy Wang's 2013 monograph, *Thinking Its Presence: Form, Race, and Subjectivity in Contemporary Asian American Poetry*; Craig Santos Perez's 2010 *Harriet* essay, "Whitewashing American Hybrid Esthetics"; Timothy Yu's 2009 *Jacket Magazine* essay, "Ron Silliman and the Ethnicization of the Avant-Garde." Yet, at the time these individual takes each appeared, they received nowhere near the same level of community attention as their more recent, scandal-centric counterparts, nor was there a widespread sense of how they all hang together as part of an ongoing critical conversation.

For better or for worse, it took the lit match of scandal for this powder keg of discourse to burst into noticeable flame. Even now, after the well-publicized conflagrations, it would be unreasonable to expect onlookers to the Goldsmith and Place controversies to possess a full sense of those controversies' recent backdrops, let alone their more distant historical precedents. That level of informedness, the charge of the literary scholar, requires a time commitment that, experience proves, can be hard to make, even for those sincere about becoming more knowledgeable about a topic. But this difficulty—that it can take years of study to obtain a thorough grasp of a critical conversation—means that when a scandal does break, the conversations that it produces can become, as Borzutsky and Heim make clear, tinged with unwitting amnesia.

In her March 15 blog post, "Thoughts on Kenneth Goldsmith and Michael Brown," the first full-length viral take on Goldsmith's performance, Jacqueline Valencia evidences this presentist orientation in response to scandal, even as she later takes care to situate her own response in a genealogy of prior responses. Citing tweets from no less than five different sources, plus providing a link to search results for mentions of Goldsmith on Twitter, the introductory section of her piece contains little of her own writing and instead reads like a *Storify* timeline of the weekend's salient events. As the piece transitions into her own paragraphed prose, the abiding sense is of someone trying to work out, with thoughtfulness, humility, respect, and mixed emotions, her complex reactions to the recently broken news.

The fundamental tension for Valencia comes from trying to square the fact that, because she considers Goldsmith "a mentor and a friend," she is inclined to be sympathetic toward his artistic ends, with the fact that she finds "the act of reading Michael Brown's autopsy report extremely problematic." Valencia ultimately criticizes the offensiveness of the poem's conceit without leveling a wholesale condemnation of Goldsmith's larger poetic practice. She closes her meditation on a fittingly open-ended and introspective note: "I must consider. I must provoke," she concludes, especially "as a woman, as a person of color, as a person of privilege and disadvantage."

In subsequent days, as reaction to her own take swells, Valencia superadds, at essay's end, two catalogs of links to other critical takes on the topic. The first, a list of "LINKS I've been reading," contains half a dozen links to antecedent takes on racism in avant-garde American poetry, including Cathy Park Hong's *Lana Turner* essay and the *Boston Review* feature, as well as the website of The Mongrel Coalition Against Gringpo, an anonymous poetry collective, formed around January 2015, that rose to prominence for its scorched earth tactics in response to the Goldsmith and Place controversies. The second catalog, a list of links to "Post-event analysis and reports," contains nine takes, a mixture of prominent and obscure ones, on Goldsmith's performance that were published in the days after Valencia's own take.

The inclusion of these hyperlinked catalogs, a move not uncommon to online takes and synopses, performs the traditional contextual function of criticism but in a way unique to the digital realm. The catalogs point to the existence of antecedent and coeval works of criticism on the topic but, as mere lists, don't work to summarize that other criticism's argumentation so as to situate the author's own arguments in a discursive constellation. Instead, the reader, in the unlikely event she has the time and willpower to read through the linked content, must connect the dots for herself.

I offer this observation descriptively, rather than as a value judgment, in order to point out a rhetorical convention of digital interpretive communities and account for the effect this convention has on critical practice. Valencia's essay constitutes an urgent, immediate, and personal reaction to Goldsmith's performance, offered in a speculative and provisional tone. It wasn't meant to be a peer-reviewed academic article and shouldn't be judged as such. But, because her essay became the first critical take to gain widespread notice, subsequent critical takes, especially in the immediately following days, came to regard her take as more absolute and authoritative, less probing and provisional, than perhaps intended.

The day after its appearance, on March 16, Valencia's take not only gets shared widely on social media but also gets cited widely in the many new critical takes that have begun to appear. Most every take that day cites Valencia's own take and at least three of them (in *Hyperallergic*, the *Inquisitr*, and the anonymous poet "dagwolf's" tumblr) cite hers at considerable length. The citations tend to emphasize the more forceful, condemnatory aspects of Valencia's critique, which has the effect of downplaying its more tentative, uncertain elements. Valencia's take, one of the first to synthesize the weekend's Twitter activity, has momentarily become the central point of reference, the *fons et origo*, in the emergent critical conversation, rather than just one node among others in a web of discourse with a complex and lengthy pre-history, a pre-history Valencia herself would later point toward in her superadded catalogs. The probing, interrogative mood of her take has, in the hands of others, quickly hardened into the voice of citational authority.

Just as quickly, however, Valencia's take becomes a mere footnote in the burgeoning conversation, just one line item among many others in the growing catalog of takes on the performance. Starting the very next day, March 17, two days after its appearance and one day after being cited everywhere and at length, Valencia's take either ceases to be mentioned in other takes (as in *The Rumpus*, *The Guardian*, and *Art in America*, to name but a few non-mentions) or, as in the introductory paragraph of Jonathan Sturgeon's take on *Flavorwire*, gets a brief, one-sentence mention, with hyperlink, in a synopsis of the notable critical responses thus far.

This rapid cycle of extensive citation then extensive non-citation, one example among many that could be adduced, illustrates the way in which scandal creates an accelerated ecosystem of self-contained response that, in its centripetal heat, can occlude important prior context. Writing from within the eye of the discursive storm, debris blowing everywhere and emotions running strong, it can feel impossible, almost beside the point, to synthesize everything that's currently being said, let alone what has been said in the recent or distant past. The point here is not that hurried criticism makes for sloppy criticism, though that may often be the case, but that timeliness has become a central value of many online interpretive communities, even traditionally slow-footed literary ones, which has in turn conditioned audience and author expectations regarding the nature of criticism. Meticulous, airtight argumentation and thorough, deeply informed contextualization become less important than economy of response and rhetorical impact, the stamina needed for a cagy twelve-round boxing match less important than the explosiveness needed to deliver a quick knockout blow to your opponent.

Even this present essay, straining against its word limit, is no exception to some of these tendencies. For all its ruminative detail and slow storytelling, the above account represents at best a partial sketch of the many recent critical conversations occasioned by Goldsmith's performance and Place's text. A full accounting of their form and content, their pre-history and post-history, would fill a book and then some. That story, more complete than the one I can tell here, would reveal even more about how and why critics operate online in the early twenty-first century and the effects of such operations on the larger literary culture. Too, that story would have much to tell about the way in which Goldsmith's Conceptual practice, in its breezy dismissal of actual reading, captures the zeitgeist of our present-day reading practices in a way that should make his proponents and detractors alike uncomfortable.

Most of all, in order to tell the full story, this hypothetical book would have to be a work of rigorous scholarship. Writing it would require thorough research, deep background knowledge about the intersections of avant-garde poetry, race, and the history of criticism, as well as careful and nuanced argumentation. In the face of such a turtle-ish, labor-intensive, and often unrewarding enterprise, it's little wonder that, on the whole, literary culture now prefers the timely provocations of the quick take, however partial, to the lumbering didacticism of the more thorough scholarly ideal. Indeed, by the time this hypothetical book was finished being researched, written, and published, the amount of careful attention it paid to recent Conceptualist controversies might well feel disproportionate to their import.

I'm not interested in valorizing either criticism or scholarship at the expense of the other. Both can do things that the other can't do in ways that are useful and necessary. But their contrasting temporal horizons, as well as their contrasting orientations toward context, offer a helpful angle of approach for understanding the import of topical criticism as practiced today. Scholarship constitutes the researched ideal toward which, in a perfect world, all criticism would tend: thorough, rigorous, complete. Scholarship recognizes that in order to understand one thing fully, it must first understand many things deeply. Criticism, more slanted toward the vernacular, doesn't deny the virtues of thoroughness but instead, like newspaper op-eds, values expediency and responsiveness on the belief that the perfect is often the enemy of the good.

The vogue for topical criticism might therefore seem harmless enough—expedient and inevitable, even—but, as it conditions audience expectations and authorial sensibilities, it erodes the middle ground between vernacular criticism and the scholarly ideal. The occupational hazard, as well as the great joy, of scholarship comes from the fact that scholars must live their greatest intellectual questions, not in a deterministically autobiographical way, but simply by carrying those questions around with them for long periods of time, *not* figuring out the answers right away, if ever, *not-*knowing where those questions are going to lead or if it will have been worth it when the scholar arrives there. That aspect of the process, a feature of any longer term writing project, isn't incompatible with the practice of criticism in general but it is incompatible with the time pressure, the cycles of relevance and irrelevance, that topical criticism exerts. It isn't actually an either-or choice between overhasty criticism and inflexibly slow scholarship—a middle ground remains possible—but it is important to recognize that the endpoint of a literary critical culture that values speed, blunt declaration, and immediate answers above all else would constitute the op-ed-ification of that culture. It would be a digital newspaper stand whose "content"—as opposed to "ideas"—was overstuffed with works of scattershot context, Swiss cheese logic, and rhetorical grandstanding. It would, in other words, be a literary culture in name alone.

Digital Palimpsesting: Literary Translation Online

Ellen Jones

We are very used, these days, to the immediacy of the Internet. Type the phrase "Google Translate" into your browser and within 0.42 seconds (or thereabouts, depending on your network speed), a familiar pair of white boxes will appear, ready to translate your foreign words as quickly as you can type them. Google's answer is always firm: there is no room for alternative translations, though the one proffered might leave much to be desired. Downloading an app allows you to speed up the process even further by skipping the typing stage: merely point your phone at a sign in a foreign language to see a real time translation. No matter how absurd, and despite phenomenal advances in algorithmic technologies the translations are often still absurd, the translated overlay still maintains an aura of authority and fixity by precisely matching the font and layout of the original sign.

Funnily enough, works of literature don't get translated in 0.42 seconds, and nor would we want them to be. Edith Grossman, best known for her translation of *Don Quixote*, claims to have spent two weeks on the first sentence alone. What's more, the decisiveness of Google's image-matched machine translations is very far from the shifting impermanence of a piece of translated literature, which may differ enormously from translator to translator. And so it might seem counter-intuitive that the Internet, besides offering us supposedly definitive translations in the blink of an eye, also lends itself to showcasing the long gestation period of a literary translation——the dozens of drafts, the myriad infinitesimal revisions and re-revisions—as well as indeterminacy and openness to change. I've come to realize that though the Internet has sped translation up via instant messaging and easily-searchable databases, there is a counter-drive among many digital publishers of literary translation to slow the process down, pulling it apart, and making its workings visible.

The web is by nature more flexible and indeterminate than paper, so texts published online have a natural malleability that stands in stark contrast to the fixity of printed material. An online publication is less like a single, settled text than like a palimpsest—a word usually used to refer to a parchment or manuscript on which one text has been partially erased and then overwritten by another text. A digital text can easily be edited at any time, even replaced with a different version. It can be linked together with other texts, made to display different sections simultaneously, or it can even vanish altogether.

Literary translation, too, is by nature malleable and open to change. There are literary classics that have been translated dozens upon dozens of times into the same language (according to Wikipedia, for instance, there have been over one hundred English versions of Dante's *Inferno*), and translators often attest that theirs is a task that never feels quite finished. So in many ways it makes sense to publish literary translation digitally. The Internet is uniquely positioned to showcase translation as an ongoing *process* rather than a finished product by allowing the linking together or layering of multiple versions of a poem or a piece of fiction. Challenging any misplaced loyalty that readers might have to a so-called "definitive version" of, say, Dante's *Inferno* (a version, of course, being by definition *not* definitive), online literary outlets encourage us to see translation as a palimpsest: a multilayered text in which each layer is both intimately connected to and separate from the others, and which, importantly, is always open to further re-inscription.

The ease and speed of digital communication have allowed conversations about literary translation—its joys, challenges, and enormous importance—to flourish in a way that is entirely unprecedented. As Scott Esposito has noted elsewhere in this volume, the key to the recent successes of literary translation is "the deterritorialized community of critics, publishers, authors, booksellers, and translators that has coalesced online." Having colleagues who, though they might live thousands of miles away, are easily contactable via the Internet represents an invaluable resource for the translator. These colleagues don't just offer support and encouragement. Sometimes even the combined forces of Word Reference, Linguee, and Urban Dictionary (even Google Street View and YouTube) aren't enough to sniff out the nuances of an unfamiliar term and find an appropriate equivalent in a new language. In these instances, simply being able to *talk* to people with different language backgrounds can be unbelievably helpful. Forums like the UK's Emerging Translators' Network or the discussion pages on the US's ALTA website can make all the difference, allowing a translator to crowdsource ideas from other translators or take the temperature of a word's particular usage in a given community of speakers. In a recent essay published in *Asymptote* on his translation of Fiston Mwanza Mujilla's novel *Tram 83*, Roland Glasser even talks about how indispensable Facebook was. It was only by picking the brains of his friends across the pond, whose vocabularies and cultural repertoires are naturally different from his own, that he was able to find a satisfying rendering for Mujilla's unusual use of the French word *biscottes*: "slim jims."

Essays like Roland's are unrivaled opportunities for readers to learn about the art of literary translation, and they are appearing increasingly often in online publications alongside translated literature. Given that online publications are unrestricted by the financial and physical limitations of a material book (there's only so much space on a page, and pages cost money to print), those who publish online are able to indulge an expansiveness that would be impractical on paper. The Internet's seemingly infinite space allows online publications to generously accommodate sophisticated dialog *about* translation in essays like Roland's that appear alongside translated literature itself.

For instance, the Editor's Note to the first edition of *Asymptote*, an online journal of international literature, stated that it would "like to be the sort of magazine where literary translation is not only presented but *also* discussed." One of the most conspicuous ways it achieves this aim is by including a translator's note with every contribution. These notes are usually between 300 and 500 words, and they allow a translator to provide greater context for the piece they have translated, especially if it has been excerpted from a longer work, or to highlight their translational goals or approach. Others use the space to talk about a specific challenge and how they have overcome this challenge. In addition, *Asymptote*'s criticism section publishes longer essays by translators about their experiences translating a recently published or forthcoming title. *Asymptote* is not alone in providing these spaces for translators' voices. A site called *Authors and Translators*, for instance, is entirely dedicated to publishing interviews (often appearing in more than one language) with authors about their translators, and with translators about their authors. The *Buenos Aires Review*, a bilingual online publication of writing from the Americas (whose manifesto echoes the manifesto of *Asymptote*: "we value translation and conversation") includes a section called "Translators' Notes." The publication *Words Without Borders Daily* has a feature called "From the Translator." Both are dedicated to translators' musings on the art of translation.

Translators are often among the most enthusiastic advocates of the literature they translate; they are also its most forensically detailed readers. For this reason their notes and essays are often both insightful and impassioned. They open a window onto the translator's daily life, detailing the considerable ingenuity, research, and meticulous editing required in translation, and showing that what's at stake in any given linguistic choice is often far greater than might be imagined. Digital publishing that allows space for this kind of discussion reminds us that literary translation doesn't just happen by magic—or by algorithm— but rather is a creative process to be respected in its own right.

I'd like to return to *Asymptote*, not just because it is the publication I know best (I've been part of the editorial team for almost three years) but also because it has, from its inception, made the most of the opportunities afforded by its digital format. The journal was conceived for publication on the Internet, and continues to operate entirely online. It is comprised of a team of multilingual editors living around the world (the senior team alone are based on three different continents). There is no centralized office space because we all communicate via the Internet and upload our content using an online project management tool. While there are naturally certain drawbacks to this system—frequent timezone snafus and the unfortunate reality of only meeting most of one's colleagues face-to-face at the occasional literary festival or book fair—the benefits enormously outweigh the disadvantages. The most obvious of these benefits is that *Asymptote* is able to provide free access to its literature anywhere in the world. Books cost money to print and to buy, and their distribution is necessarily limited by geography, and these two factors combine to lock many people out of the kinds of conversations we want to be having. By operating online, however, the journal is able to have experts all around the world pull emerging and established writers (who might otherwise have remained unknown to English speakers) out of different international literary scenes and give them a global readership.

Asymptote has also taken advantage of digital publishing where its content is concerned. For one thing, it has consistently imbricated literary translation with critical and reflective commentary. But it has also pushed the simultaneous publication of multiple linked versions of a text in new innovative directions, demonstrating a commitment to displaying translation as *process*. In fact, a typical contribution to *Asymptote* exists in at least three versions: the original language, the English translation, and the audio version. Typically these will also be accompanied by an illustration commissioned by a guest artist, and by a note from the translator. The online format enables interactivity between these different modes and media, facilitating a double or triple reading, as visitors to the site can move between the hyper-linked versions or read while listening to a recording in the original language.

While the majority of contributions to *Asymptote* are trans-lated into English, texts of particular significance are translated into other languages too, to make them available as widely as possible. For example, in 2013 the journal published Jonas Hassen Khemiri's "Open Letter to Beatrice Ask"—*in twenty different languages*. These included Basque and Indonesian as well as major European and Asian languages. Khemiri's letter was originally published in the Swedish newspaper *Dagens Nyheter* in March 2013, and addressed to the Swedish Minister of Justice, Beatrice Ask. It condemns the practice of racial profiling by Swedish police and Ask's recent refusal to take the matter seriously. Though the letter had already broken a record for the most widely shared publication in Sweden, *Asymptote* was able to maintain that momentum and increase it. Making it available in so many different languages meant that international media outlets all over the world—the *New York Times*, France's *Courrier International*, Italy's *La Citta Nuova*, Japan's *Tosho Shimbun*—also began to pay attention.

Setting aside the political importance of making Khemiri's letter more widely available for a moment, what's also notable about this publishing strategy is that it makes it impossible to forget that what we're reading is a translation. Publishers of print books are often reluctant to market literary translations as *translations*—in fact, it's still easy for a reader to get through a book in English with little awareness of or engagement with its provenance in another language. Only in recent years have translators' names occasionally appeared on book jackets. *Asymptote* strives for the opposite state of affairs, whereby readers are reminded at every turn that the text they are reading has passed through another language, and are asked to think about what that process might entail. So, whichever translation of Khemiri's letter we are reading—Slovenian, Greek, or Traditional Chinese—on the right hand side of the page are hyperlinks to the other nineteen versions and the biographies of all their translators. The versions are layered and bound together in a digital palimpsest that refuses to let us forget that any given translation will always be provisional and will just be one among a nexus of different iterations.

I want to offer specific examples of other digital palimpsests that chart a trajectory across different languages, modes, and media, and that incorporate critique of translation into translations themselves. Each of these appears in an online publication that showcases and interrogates translation's processes, encouraging readers to think through the relationships between a given text and its various antecedents or subsequent versions.

The first appears in *Words Without Borders*, a monthly online magazine of literature in English translation that publishes many (but not all) of its pieces bilingually. As in *Asymptote*, readers can often listen to an audio recording of the original and easily click from one text version to the other. An added feature means it is also possible to view both versions in parallel columns on the same page. Although readers might not understand both languages, being able to contemplate the visual differences between versions—different scripts, different uses of accents or cedillas, different paragraph lengths or punctuation—makes an unfamiliar language take on a certain substance. No longer located in a nebulous "elsewhere," the original text is present in a way that cannot be ignored.

Takako Arai's "Wheels," a poem about a three-generation-old ghost that haunts a spinning factory, was published in *Words Without*

Borders in October 2016. It appears in Arai's original Japanese and in an English translation by Jeffrey Angles, accompanied by a video of the author-translator pair giving a bilingual reading. All three versions can be viewed simultaneously on a single page. In the video, we hear Arai reading a few lines in Japanese, followed by Angles reading his translation of the same few lines in English, and so on throughout the poem in a constant back and forth. This forces us to slow our reading down and never forget that the poem was originally composed in Japanese. Those who watch the video *and* read the English text will also notice that Angles's translation shifts considerably between the two. In the video version, almost every single line is subtly different to the written version. For instance, these lines in which the ghost warns that a fire is about to break out:

Text version	*It's coming! It'll be here tonight!*
	It is out? It is out yet?
	Has someone smothered it?
Video version:	*It's coming tonight! It'll be here tonight!*
	Did you extinguish it? Did you put it out?
	Did you smother it?

Elsewhere, whole phrases are omitted and sentences rearranged entirely. These differences underscore not only the mutable, ephemeral nature of the oral mode—every spoken reading of this poem will differ in its delivery—but also of the translation itself, which remains open to future changes. For those of us who do not read Japanese, they make us wonder whether Angles's spoken version is different from his written version because Arai's spoken version is different from her written version—or whether the variation exists solely between the English versions. They make us want to find out why Angles has made certain choices and why he appears to change his mind. Each version is intimately connected to and yet different from its siblings, each haunts the others just like the poem's ghost haunts the girls in the factory, just like the echo of the poem's repeated refrain— which is slightly altered—and weaves through later stanzas, reinforcing the poem's rhythm and momentum. The impression is of a text that could continue shifting, like the spinning wheel in the poem's final lines, *"on and on to the end of time."*

My second example is taken from *The Creative Literary Studio*, an online publication that celebrates the art of text making. Its submission criteria state that the editors' primary interest is in "exploring the process of text making," and for this reason contributors are encouraged to include commentaries on why and how their writing has developed in a particular way. Although it also features work written originally in English, translation makes up a large part of the publication, which shows special interest in the links between translation and creative writing. Recent contributions have included, for instance, essays by translators, bilingual texts published in facing page translations, translations in which the original texts are available via hyperlink, and visual translations from text to image.

A piece of writing by the Mexican novelist and essayist Valeria Luiselli illustrates the publication's focus on translation as process with particular clarity. Her collection of essays *Papeles falsos* appeared in English as *Sidewalks* in 2014, translated by Christina MacSweeney. The excerpt from it, in which Luiselli reflects on "relingos"—silences or empty spaces—showcases different stages of that work's migration from Spanish into English. The excerpt appears in Word document format, the format in which the translation was composed before being typeset by the publisher. It includes passages of highlighted text marking queries, changes, and work in progress, and it includes MacSweeney's margin comments in Word's "track changes" feature.

This enhanced, palimpsestuous version of *Sidewalks* constitutes a new work in its own right, one that blurs the lines between creative and critical writing and emphasizes the contingent nature of translation. MacSweeney's comments draw readers' attention to the kinds of decisions she and Luiselli had to make during the production of the translation. For instance: when is it necessary to supplement the translated text with details about a person or place, in order to avoid distancing new readers who might be unfamiliar with the cultural context? Should certain words be kept in Spanish, and, if so, what effect this might have on readers? Above all, the excerpt makes clear the degree to which the translation is a collaborative effort between the two women, by telling us where they agreed or disagreed, and when it was the author herself (whose English is extremely good) who came up with the solution to a translational problem. By noting what they (and their editor) were reading at the time of translation (Roland Barthes), and by pointing out connections to other writers (Walter Benjamin) and to Luiselli's other published work (2012's *Faces in the Crowd*), MacSweeney depicts translation as a *conversation* between the text being translated, other texts, and other agents. The text looks hectic and chaotic, and very much in flux.

It's important to note that this composite excerpt in *The Creative Literary Studio* has actually been very self-consciously put together. MacSweeney's annotations and highlights are not "original" para-texts, to use Gérard Genette's terminology, but "posthumous" ones—which is to say, the version of the text published here is not an early draft of a work in progress, but rather a polished translation to which annotations have latterly been added. By presenting a finished and carefully curated work that nonetheless gives the impression of being fluid, MacSweeney turns the processes of translation itself into a work of art, making an esthetic virtue of the semblance of instability and uncertainty.

My final example returns to *Asymptote*, and the piece *River | Horse | Haiku*. This piece comprises four poems by the Japanese writer Nenten Tsubouchi, published in January 2016 in *Asymptote*, each poem translated by Martin Rock and Joe Pan into as many as ten different multimedia versions. Tsubouchi's original haiku are written in Kanji. Above each one, in smaller type, is a version in *furigana*, a phonetic alphabet that indicates the proper pronunciation of the ideogrammatic Kanji. There follows a transliteration of the Kanji into Roman script, accompanied by a superscript homophonic or "surface" translation into English as a playful counterpart to the *furigana*. For instance:

はるかぜ るかぜr iはは はiし はかぜr りゅうかくさん ゅうかくさんnsち
春風に母死ぬ龍角散が散り

How're you, Cassini? Ha ha! (she knew). Are you coxswain?
Got cheery.
harukaze ni haha shinu ryûkakusan ga chiri

These "surface translations," along with the original Japanese, are also accessible as audio recordings read aloud by the translators. The surface translations sound comically Anglicized. It's worth noting that the audio recordings change the order so the Japanese is read before the homophonic English, emphasizing the exchangeability of versions and lack of hierarchy among them. From the ultra-concision of the haiku form, an abundance of English variants then spring: at least three different translations of each poem follow, all typographically distinct. This allows the translators to showcase the poems' many ambiguities and complexities, including the compound make-up of many Japanese words. For instance, as Martin Rock has explained in an interview, the word for snowflake (牡丹雪) is a compound of the kanji for "peony" (牡丹) and the one for "snow" (雪), while "peony" is itself made up of the kanji for "male animal" (牡) and the one for "red earth" (丹). Each haiku is then further represented in a "diagrammatic translation" that synthesizes in words and images the various possible denotations of each original ideogram. Contrary to the popular understanding of translation as inevitable loss or diminishment, here it makes meaning proliferate through repetition and variation.

In addition to the usual translator's note, each haiku is followed by its own short commentary in the form of a prose poem, which, as the translators explain, "in itself is a creative and relational work acting simultaneously in the mode of explanation and the mode of creation," much like MacSweeney's annotations on Luiselli's essay. This extensive "versioning" imposes a mode of reading that could only be possible online, one that alternates between text, audio, and image. By incorporating the translator's commentary into the work itself, Rock and Pan dissolve the boundaries between the literary and the critical texts, bringing together those twin goals established in *Asymptote*'s first issue—translation and conversation—to suggest that the latter is an integral part of the former.

These examples suggest that, despite the immediacy with which the Internet now allows us to communicate—and to translate—digital publishing often has the opposite effect of slowing reading down. Our progress through Luiselli's essay is periodically interrupted by MacSweeney's annotations; Angles's translation of Arai's poem is slowed down by half when we listen to the bilingual reading; and Rock and Pan force us to read Tsubouchi's haiku over and over and over again. This slow reading allows us time to think through the relationships between one version of a published work and its antecedents, drawing attention to the processes of a text's development.

Digital magazines and journals offer a larger, more inclusive space for translations that are expansive and self-reflexive, building dialog into each contribution in order to increase our understanding of what literary translation actually *is*, and to heighten respect for the skill and creativity it involves. They are turning the palimpsestuous processes of translation into art works in their own right: compositions that can be flexed and stretched, and which are accepting of change, rather than purporting to reach any kind of end-point.

Futurebook Critics and Cultural Curators in a Socially Networked Age

Anna Kiernan

Literary editors used to compare curating the books pages in a news-paper to "putting on a good dinner party," in which a rich mix of authors would jostle for space at a lavishly laden table, according to James Curran's article "Literary Editors, Social Networks and Cultural Traditions" published in 2000. How things have changed. Few authors now enjoy the luxury of retreating to their ivory towers to write—they must also engage socially, connect with communities, and tweet. The role of reviewers has also radically changed. Getting paid to write reviews, let alone to attend literary lunches and to flat-plan review pages, is an increasingly rarefied role enjoyed by the few, and which is being challenged by the many new influencers, profes-sional bloggers, and free reviewers on the block.

Literary critics, like many other arts reviewers, have been adversely affected by the decline of print sales and the growing ava-lanche of digital content. The quality press in the UK has cut back on critical writing about the arts, with *The Independent on Sunday* drop-ping "The Critics" section in 2013 and *The Telegraph* halving its arts budget in 2008 and then cutting its head of arts in 2016. *The Guardian* has also cut back on its roster of staff reviewers, while continuing to grow its profile as a go-to site for podcasts, book groups, and the ongoing business project of repurposing at-risk expertise through the *Guardian* masterclass program. Tom Gatti, arts editor at the *New Statesman* told me that, "The volume of work has increased and the quantity of emails, pitches and releases has become suffocating." So the trend towards creating umbrella roles for arts editors (in which the remit is to oversee all arts coverage rather than to lead on a specific cultural output) adds to the sense among some critics that theirs is an art-form that is undervalued, under-resourced, and under siege.

In 2014, Reuters' research institute published a report titled "Anyone Can Be a Critic: Is There Still a Need for Professional Arts and Culture Journalism in the Digital Age?" What, then, is the point of critics? What do they bring to the party that a debate on Goodreads, Amazon, or Wattpad doesn't? And how has criticism adapted to the digital age? More than fifty-six percent of review coverage from the quality press in the UK is published digitally first or only on digital, according to Jarkoo Jokelainen in his Reuters report. This means that while engagement with online review sites such as Goodreads (which may draw on expert opinion but which are powered by peer-to-peer reviews) is in excess of twenty-five million. Professional cultural review coverage has also increased, as the continuing success of the "online only" arts desk attests.

In this chapter, I'll discuss the anatomy of a review and will consider some of the ways in which the future of reviewing aligns with the future of books, in all its complex, creative, and multi-platformed possibilities. In an era of digitization, book publishing's ability to produce beautiful material objects and personalized narrative experiences are key to its ongoing success. The *Bookseller* magazine's enterprising Futurebook project is concerned with ingraining innovation, change management and trend spotting in book publishing. And as book publishing embraces the new, so book critics must too.

◆ ◆ ◆

In "Literary Editors, Social Networks and Cultural Traditions," James Curran maps out some of the ways in which the cultural hierarchy bears upon the book world, through his examination of the quality press's review sections. When Curran interviewed eleven literary editors of national newspapers and weekly periodicals he discovered that a "stock response" was that "literary editors merely respond . . . to the external world." They deciphered a "pre-set agenda shaped by what readers are interested in, and what is being talked about" alongside a need to cover new works by important authors, with established reputations, and with track records. More confusingly—and this is the nub of Curran's findings—literary editors appeared to be unclear about what it was, exactly, that they did, despite believing their roles to be well-defined. Curran found that the rationales given for selecting particular titles was particularly confounding, given that many critics "invoked a theory of predestination in which books were not chosen but chose themselves," while others, "summoned an image of improvisation and randomness . . . governed by instinct and insight, without a clear pattern."

This rather vague and instinctive sense of what literary editors do is quite different from the expectations of the form (of reviewing) itself. In his 1937 article "Criticism Inc.," John Crowe Ransom outlined the "rules" of criticism. Reviews, he argued, should be objective and there should be a synopsis and paraphrasing, comparison, linguistics, moral studies, and assimilation. He went on to say that, "The reviewer has a job of presentation and interpretation as well as criticism. The most we can ask of him is that he know when the criticism begins, and that he make it as clean and definitive as his business permits."

This sense of the critic being responsible and informed chimes with film critic Mark Kermode's claim for his craft: "What matters is that you wade through the good, the bad, and the ugly, all year round, producing accountable reviews that combine pithily expressed opinion, description, contextualization, analysis and (at best) entertainment, in whatever medium."

Written almost a hundred years apart, Kermode and Ransom's insights have much in common. Both infer the need for objectivity (which, in unregulated digital forums, is not enforceable, and which has resulted in a lot of "paid for" review content). Both recognize the importance of good writing, differentiating between opinion and facts (the hard news element of the review) and the value of interpretation. But where Kermode differs is in his view that reviews should entertain and in his acknowledgement that medium matters.

And what's even more striking about these sketches of the role of the critic and the function of review is that none of them mention the reader.

Social interactions with influencers, who include bloggers, vloggers, publishers, and of course writers has, for the most part, become more appealing to readers than being held at arm's length by highfalutin' cultural critics. Bringing us back to the question that almost all publications face now, which is why would readers pay for content when they can read what they need for free? As social media marketer Mark Fidelman asserts, "For me, there are no 'professional' critics that matter anymore. In our new social world, the crowd must decide."

I am writing as the year in which "the crowd decided" is drawing to a close, a year in which "the crowd" voted in favor of Brexit and Donald Trump. And so for this and other reasons, I'm a little skeptical about the crowd deciding, since it seems to be opening the floodgates of decision-making based on the lowest common denominator. But the disruptive vigor in Fidelman's statement, and the impulse, as it were, to reclaim territory (or even to *appear* to reclaim territory) that has previously been demarcated for the culturally elite, is telling, signifying as it does a dissatisfaction with "how things are" and a seeming desire to democratize the mode of production of literary reception.

But let's see what this phenomenon looks like on closer inspection. A case in point is Kiran Desai's 2006 novel *The Inheritance of Loss*. Critically lauded, the novel won the Man Booker Prize and the National Book Critics Circle Award for Fiction. The reviews it garnered on Amazon were, by contrast, mixed. Daniel Allington undertook qualitative analysis of professional reviewers' reviews and compared them to customer reviews. His research showed that customer reviews were more likely to criticize the novel for its characters and less likely to discuss its political themes. The other glaring problem for Amazon reviews is the fake review phenomenon, whereby reviews are sold on Fiverr.com to promote specific authors and texts, though Amazon has apparently been cracking down on fake reviews since 2015. By emphasizing the "likeability" of key characters, customer reviews tend to celebrate the moment of emotional connection between characters that so often forms the touchstone of relatable storylines, as opposed to engaging with more complex questions raised through discussions of political themes, moral ambiguity, and experiments with form, just some of the characteristics which differentiate literary fiction from genre fiction.

This tendency is also characteristic of the way in which book groups discuss their book choices (which I discuss further in my 2011 essay "The Growth of Reading Groups as a Feminine Leisure Pursuit: Cultural Democracy or Dumbing Down?"), which perhaps goes some way to explain the popularity of reading groups for the fifty-six percent of American women who read at least one book a month. Book groups are a place where readers feel comfortable sharing their views—which is why the online equivalents are so popular. Such discussions are based on the *appreciation* of literature, rather than on its critical evaluation, which has prompted some hostile reactions from the literary elite. Books selected for Richard and Judy's television Book Club, or for that matter Oprah's Book Club (1996-2011), for instance, relied on a very particular set of criteria that reflected those listed by Malcolm Gladwell in his discussion of the success of

The Divine Secrets of the Ya-Ya Sisterhood in *The Tipping Point* (2000), Gladwell defined a "book group" book as being "emotionally sophisticated, character-driven, multi-layered [and which] invites reflection and discussion." What is notable here is that, historically, criticism serves a different purpose and the measure of critically acceptable criticism is at odds with Malcolm Gladwell's criteria for a book group book, which is also applicable to customer generated and peer-to-peer reviews on Amazon and Goodreads.

Peter Stothard, chair of the Booker Prize in 2012 and previously editor of both *The Times* and *The Times Literary Supplement*, seems to be largely in favor of the authority of the elite critic. His unremitting view is that blogs about books pose a threat to literary criticism (seen by him as a purveyor of difficult ideas to the general reader). His appointment to chair the Booker followed on from that of Stella Rimington, former director general of the M15, whom he distanced himself from with reference to her ideal Booker submission being "readable."

"If we make the main criteria good, page-turning stories—if we prioritize unargued opinion over criticism—then I think literature will be harmed," Stothard told *The Independent*. "Someone has to stand up for the role and the art of the critic, otherwise it will just be drowned—overwhelmed. And literature will be worse off." Could "unargued opinion" be construed as "appreciation"? If so, Stothard's view aligns with Ransom's, who similarly delineates between "appreciation, which is private, and criticism, which is public" as a means of articulating the importance of the seemingly remote aesthete and intellectual over the so-called "general" (and often female) reader.

But while the tension between high culture and the assertion of value through the well-worn channels attributed to the connected and the elite seem to have changed little in more than a century in some quarters, in other, arguably more connected communities, Stothard's views seem snobbish and unreconstructed. Simon Savidge, reviewer and book blogger for Waterstones and at *Savidge Reads: The Chronicles of a Book Addict,* responded by saying that he found Stothard's views, "disheartening . . . I think anyone who reads a lot, just by reading, has the ability to critique anything they read . . ."

Book publishing, and the marketing and publicity which surrounds the event of publication, has shifted its emphasis too. There has been much debate about how digital books have undercut print over the past decade, fueled in part by tensions resulting from Google's digitization project, Amazon's domination of the e-book project, and the shift in perception and sales around self-publishing. Thankfully, this oppositional discourse has moved on to make space for more creative possibilities emerging from the digital landscape, in which the most powerful advocates, compelling campaigns, and influential cultural intermediaries sometimes emerge from unexpected places and through unexpected people. This view is shared by arts editors such as Tom Gatti from the *New Statesman,* who told me that, "In terms of the literary landscape, the work of small presses and university presses has become increasingly interesting as the big publishers, particularly in recent years, have become a bit more conservative."

Visual Editions is a good example of a different model for publishing. Run by graphic designer Anna Gerber and advertising strategist Britt Iverson, Visual Editions was set up to create a "new kind of story experience." Many of its titles are both innovative in terms of form and narrative and some, such as *Composition No. 1* seem to invite the reviewer to engage with the texts in disruptive, playful ways *Composition No. 1,* for instance, could be shuffled like playing cards and, as a result, the narrative could be read and reviewed in an infinite number of ways. Jonathan Safran Foer was so inspired by the story *The Street of Crocodiles* (1992) by Bruno Schulz that he carved a new narrative out of Schulz's text, cutting out words to create his concrete poetry-inspired *Tree of Codes* (2010). Visual Editions' challenge was to find a printer willing to use a different die-cut for every page, a process which was captured in a gorgeously shot and soundtracked film which features on their website. Each element of the creative process became part of a self-perpetuating literary lineage, which was documented, shared, and reviewed at each stage. Intriguingly, this rich collaborative venture takes as its starting-point the ultimate form of artistic appreciation: the homage.

Penned in the Margins, which publishes "risk-taking" literary work and programs "pioneering live literature" also traverses the space between literary creation and appraisal, most notably in Hannah Silva's one-woman show, *Schlock!* Silva's strange and beautiful performance uses sound, dance, readings and sign language to share a journey through sexuality, loss, and language. The opening scene signifies the most savage of reviews—destroying the text, as Silva calmly rips out the pages from *Fifty Shades of Gray*. Throughout the show, Silva's lyrical lament for the loss of Kathy Acker, literary anti-heroine and "high priestess of punk," is in stark contrast to her judgement of E.L. James' sexually reductive genre fiction, which forms an ideologically charged discursive stance characteristic of comparative reviewing.

The idea of authors performing their texts to new audiences, and expanding their narratives across art-forms and, indeed, space, has injected a much-needed jolt of life into an industry that is at times a little late to the party. For instance, when Nikesh Shukla's book was due for publication with HarperCollins, Shukla decided to approach promoting *Meatspace* by launching a piece of meat into space. He attached a GoPro camera to a lamb chop, attaching them both to a weather balloon powered by helium, with GPS tracking, and then he shared the footage online.

The response on social media was, according to the author, unprecedented and "unmanageable" (the video has been viewed 300,000 times on YouTube). And the result was that the book gained traction and promoted the writer's career, giving him the kind of "status" that resulted in him being "a writer people . . . think of when they're programming things." By playing out the concept of his novel in this curatorially inventive way, Shukla engaged with new digital audiences and intrigued traditional reviewers. The critics said that "the novel captures a cultural moment" (*Guardian*) and described it as "an anarchic, self-involved and admirably honest portrait of a bookish life lived in the brave new digital world" (*New Statesman*). None, however, saw fit to launch their reviews into space.

The Bookseller magazine's Futurebook awards, which recognize companies and individuals who are driving the publishing industry forward, shortlisted Novel Effect, Publishizer, Joosr, Kadaxis, and StoryTourist for best book tech in 2016. Kadaxis, which uses data science to connect people with books, won. Its sister company AuthorCheckpoint makes its living from providing authors with the kind of data, algorithms, and comparisons with bestsellers that can then inform authorial decisions such as how many "difficult" sentences to include and how many passive sentences to allow.

The role of authors, it would seem, is now subject to increasingly detailed, often contractual demands, in terms of market expectations and promotional obligations. In *Merchants of Culture: The Publishing Business in the Twenty-First Century* (2010), John B. Thompson noted that, at book proposal stage, publishers now want their authors to engage digitally: "for in the Internet age, these new forms of online marketing are becoming more and more decisive in shaping the visibility of books and their fate."

While Curran's research on bookish social networks revealed a lack of clarity about the role of the literary editor, literary editors today, who work in an increasingly pressurized environment, seem to have a clearer sense of what their job entails. When selecting books to review, Gatti concludes that "Fiction is much harder to navigate, but I try to steer a course between the big guns (writers like Zadie Smith and Ian McEwan) and the intriguing outliers from small presses or innovative writers."

AuthorCheckpoint offers one more way for writers to prime their writing for the new mainstream mediated marketplace. But such carefully crafted genre fictions, which may well be popular on Goodreads may not be the most groundbreaking books. The challenge for future critics and cultural curators now is not only to seek out the finest stories across platforms but also to challenge themselves. What are critics doing differently, via digital or print, that brings the critical practice into the arena of Futurebooks in ways that will connect with the communities with whom they want to share great literature and berate slack writing? Readers will find the level of insight they seek online, be it paid for reviews on Amazon or arresting, astutely paired text and image on *The White Review*'s website. It's only really the publishing projects which operate beyond the text, in immersive or exploratory multimedia ways, that will make the practice of traditional book reviewing as creatively relevant as the best of what we review. As novelist Joanne Harris (@Joannechocolat) recently put it in her #TenTweetsOnGettingReviews, "Review as you would like to be reviewed: honestly and intelligently. Remember: no-one owes you anything."

Publishing As Criticism: Managing Textual Superabundance

Michael Bhaskar

Arguably the most salient property of the digital literary universe is the not the changed behavior of text but its overwhelming abundance. With the coming of digital networks we have seen probably the most radical inflection in terms of the amount of available text ever produced, and certainly the most drastic since Gutenberg. Yes, it's a cliché; and no, that doesn't mean it isn't true.

People have always felt there was too much to read. It's a complaint as old as reading itself. Plato famously didn't even trust written text. Hippocrates quipped that while the arts are long, life is short. Seneca said "the abundance of books is a distraction" and even the Bible weighed in via Ecclesiastes 12:12: "Of making books there is no end." The Library of Alexandria is estimated to have contained some 500,000 papyrus scrolls at its peak, an abundance far beyond the mastery of any one individual.

But this wasn't an exclusively European phenomenon. One ninth century Baghdadi bookseller, Ibn al-Nadim, created a bibliography of 3,500 Arabic authors and all of their texts. In the Byzantine Empire, in China, and in the Islamic world similar complaints were felt long before the rise of the press. Lack of advanced reproductive technologies did not, in short, mean we felt our literary lives were impoverished.

Nonetheless the fifteenth-century launch of European printing was still a sea change. The great early printers, including names like Koberger, Manutius, and Plantin, ran quasi-industrial operations using highly trained teams across multiple presses. There was also the discovery of ancient texts from Greece and Rome, a huge spur to the amount of information available. Then the "discovery» of the New World led to a huge boom in sources of knowledge and writing. And of course the Reformation was fought through printed pamphlets whose numbers mushroomed in line with the intensity of social and theological debate. Even that great reformer John Calvin had cause to complain of "that confused forest of books." In the wake of printing, everyone from Leibniz ("that horrible mass of books which keeps on growing...; the indefinite multitude of authors will shortly expose them all to the danger of general oblivion") to Boswell ("this teeming of the press in modern times") felt the urge to complain of *multitudo librorum*, the overabundance of books.

In the words of the Harvard scholar Ann Blair: "We describe ourselves as living in an information age as if this were something completely new. In fact, many of our current ways of thinking about and handling information descend from patterns of thought and practices that extend back for centuries." If the best minds from history have always felt textually overwhelmed, is today really so different?

Yes, for the simple reason that the resources needed to publish text have dropped to virtually zero. This is historically unprecedented, and we are still grappling with the results. Every week there is a new study of Big Data, replete with mind-blowing statistics: that the rate of data growth is sixty percent a year; that Facebook churns multiples of the Library of Congress daily; that each American is bombarded with the equivalent of 175 newspapers' worth of information every day; that we have created more data in the past two years than in the rest of human history put together. It's all impressive. Most of it doesn't have anything to do with literature or writing, but it's all part of the same dynamic that is re-ordering our experience of the world: that creating, storing, and transmitting data, information and even knowledge is materially cheaper and easier than at any other point in human history, not by a small amount but by a vast gulf.

The number of books available is caught in this dynamic. Books with ISBNs, a shorthand for books "officially" published, has hit one million a year in the English language. Yet this completely underestimates the amount of books being published thanks to self-publishing platforms like Kindle Direct Publishing, or the impact of short-run and print-on-demand technology, or the countless stories being written on websites like Wattpad, or simply circulating amongst friends.

We've complained for millennia about having too much to read. But this time it's really true. The Japanese even have a word for it: *tsundoku*, the feeling of having too many books to read. More than anything else the textual universe of the twenty-first century is defined by a superabundance underwritten by digital technology and the promise of limitless publishing capacity.

In most discussions of literary criticism the publishing of a book is lost. While the history of the book has made huge strides in re-introducing a material component to our understanding of literature, it has focused less on the processual, cultural, and financial elements involved in the *publishing* of a book, an activity quite distinct from the act of producing a finished object or even a digital file, and more on the making of the codex.

Nonetheless publishing studies has been around for quite a few years. On one side it came from bibliographic studies—the painstaking work that goes into establishing the history of books and texts. On the other side it came from professional education. Publishing departments at universities and colleges were made to effectively train new generations of publishers. Either way, the scope of the academic study of publishing tends to be narrow: either pragmatically oriented or focused on the minutiae of a text's history.

Why should that be so? The rest of literary and communication studies has, for decades, been through a series of revolutions that saw the size and the scope of their fields of enquiry change dramatically. Moreover publishing itself, far from the (relatively) static objects of enquiry that concern literary scholars (namely, books), has been in a constant state of flux, never more so than in the years of the new millennium which coincided with the Web 2.0 boom and the digital revolution. If publishing studies is still a recent discipline in its modern form, then now we are seeing an even newer one: publishing theory. It asks the big, difficult, abstract but essential questions.

This matters as textual superabundance is in fact publishing superabundance. Thanks to the open nature of digital networks, publishing has been democratized and turbocharged; hence the radical surfeit of texts. If we are to understand that surfeit, we have to understand publishing. We need better theories of publishing, of what it is, how it works, why it's changing, and what it does in the world. And if we need better theories of digital publishing, we need a better understanding of publishing in the first place.

Something else that's often forgotten amongst literary critics is that publishing is also a process of criticism. Indeed, it is the first external act of criticism bestowed on a work. In that sense it is the foundational exegesis. By the time critics of any kind get to a work, it has already been critiqued: by the publisher. The act of publishing constitutes a profound form of literary criticism that has been under appreciated by critics, scholars, and even publishers themselves. The overall positioning of a book is the responsibility of a publisher and in every such act there is necessarily an interpretation involved, explicitly designed to shape subsequent readings.

The Cambridge critic Andy Martin spent a year working with one of the world's bestselling novelists, Lee Child. Martin watched Child in the process of writing a novel, literally hanging off his shoulder as the words were tapped out; watching a novel unfold in real time, words on the page direct from the author, with no intermediaries. It's clear from the process that both Child and Martin were able in this format to have views of the work very different from those of popular perception. Martin, for example, imagined a Cambridge exam based on what he had learned: "ENGLISH TRIPOS Part II; Paper 12 Lee Child Studies":

'SECTION A

Discuss ONE of the following. Candidates must draw on the oeuvre of Lee Child in the context of other writers and forms of culture.

i.   "Literature does not exist. Or if it does, it's a hoax or a delusion."

ii. "Writing is insignificant in comparison with the voice."

iii. "The history of Western literature is essentially a history of the knight errant."

iv. EITHER: "Narrative provides human beings with a tool for survival—or a weapon." OR: "All narrative is a sign of primordial failure and disappointment."

v.   "Every book exists in order to be made into a film."

vi. "The writer is a neurotic sociopath in need of psychoanalysis."

It's clear from these arch questions that Martin has a good deal of experience in setting literature exams. But it's also a provocative exercise in re-assessing Lee Child, not now as a thriller writer, suitable for tired businessman to read on another long haul flight, but as a writer in a grand tradition, a fruitful discussion piece for Cambridge tutorials alongside a George Eliot or even a James Joyce. This is an amusing, different kind of approach to criticism—perhaps weird, but not wholly implausible.

Reimagining Child in this way is a nightmare for a publisher of popular mass-market paperbacks. Everything they do is to disrupt this; to position the book as for the airport, as thriller, as "bestseller," as disposable good, as pop culture. As much as anything else, it's the publisher that makes Jack Reacher novels what they are, not Lee Child.

The point is that publishers do not *want* Lee Child to be studied. He is read in prisons because his prose is easy. It has a spare and lapidary quality, something of Hemingway, of Camus, even Pinter ("Reacher said nothing.") But, of course, those are precisely the comparisons the publisher never makes. Child himself is the first to admit, being labeled as a "commercial" pulp writer is not always where he sees himself. But this is where the publishers have placed him. The only admissible commercial interpretation of his work is as genre thriller, and, by taking the publisher's advance, Child becomes complicit.

How do publishers act as critics? In almost every interaction there is an element of this but I will focus on three in particular: editing, design, and pricing.

What else is an edit than a criticism? To Lord Byron it was a "gelding"; to Henry James, "that butcher's trade." Blake Morrison has likened Percy Bysshe Shelley's edits to Mary Shelley's *Frankenstein* to "a kind of rape"; Vladimir Nabokov thought editors "pompous avuncular brutes." Yet, especially at the structural level, editing is all about critiquing a work, improving it, changing the spin and weighting of it. Edits can be broad or insanely detailed, but either way they put certain glosses or interpretations on a work, shaping it to the editor's vision. Every edit is an instantiation of an editor's reading. Because the editor's work is then invisible, buried behind the author's name, this potentially vast initial act of criticism is almost always erased. And yet it is powerfully present in every subsequent encounter.

In a brilliant essay on the art of editing, the writer Blake Morrison discusses how important the editing process was to major twentieth century works including Eliot's *The Wasteland* and Scott Fitzgerald's *The Great Gatsby*. The editor on that novel was Max Perkins, one of the greatest editors of all time. He changed everything about the book. The original two choices of title now seem extraordinarily dubious: either *Among the Ash-Heaps and Millionaires* or *Trimalchio in West Egg*. Perkins insisted on the instantly more resonant *The Great Gatsby*. He also insisted the novel have an additional 10,000 words. The first draft of 50,000 words felt light to Perkins. The end result feels just right, still short but not a novella. It was Perkins who thought Gatsby himself needed fleshing out, even suggesting such details as the phrase "old sport," now the tic we associate most with Gatsby. Scott Fitzgerald paid tribute to these multiple interventions saying it was only after encountering Perkins that he "sat down and wrote something I was proud of."

Morrison traces a long running battle between D.H. Lawrence and his editor, Edward Garnett. When published, *Sons and Lovers* was some 10,000 words shorter thanks to Garnett's cuts. Lawrence, and subsequent scholars, were not impressed, seeing this, in Lawrence's own words, as a "mangling" of the text. Yet in my experience as an editor, publisher, and writer such controversies are rare; most of the time almost any book is more successful post-edit. Even before an acquisitions meeting, a whole team of readers will have read, commented on, and shaped the work. The text that is finally read by readers is often unrecognizable. This is an active form of criticism; criticism in real time and real life.

Publishers also know that everyone judges a book by its cover. Even critics. It's almost impossible to read a book without this reading being inflected by the visual identity ascribed to a book. Why else do publishers spend money and time, and have a lot of arguments, over covers? It's a book's first sales pitch. It tells people what it's like and why they should buy it. Just as an editor will have a vision for a book, so publishers explicitly design books to be like another writer; to clearly sit in a certain genre or even on a specific bookshelf. Think of the difference between a cover from Gallimard in France and an equivalent UK publisher, say a Jonathan Cape or Faber and Faber. Gallimard covers are all generally of one piece. They are not illustrated. They have a set layout and typography: austere, high minded, learned, solemn. The template gestures towards the publishing forms of the eighteenth and nineteenth centuries. It situates new books, even radically contemporaneous works, as part of a grand European tradition of literary writing where, quite specifically, it is the writing itself that is paramount. The text needs no accompanying image, will not be reduced to something approximating an advert.

By contrast, what might be termed the "Anglo–Saxon" school of cover design has no such qualms. Virtually every book is accorded a unique cover, which is strongly "visual" (rather than simply textual), and which does in some way act as an advert for the book, which is quite explicitly designed as a commercial signal for the book's content. Only books that are accorded classic status through the still mysterious process of canon formation get a classic jacket. When the singer Morrissey shortcut this process by publishing his *Autobiography* as a Penguin Classic he hit a wall of protest. Even here, of course, that instantly identifiable Classics cover is an interpretation; one almost no one else thought valid for Morrissey's book.

Every cover is an act of criticism, a reading. The challenge for covers is how to accommodate multiple readings. Take a writer who works on many levels like John Le Carré. He is at once author of major modern classics. But he is also a popular genre writer of spy fiction and cold war thrillers. Yet he might be seen as a major literary author exploring the structures of power and commerce in a post-moral late-capitalist world. Hence he needs multiple jackets and multiple editions. He has classy Penguin Modern Classics, in the recognizable formula, with atmospheric photography; he has film adaptation jackets with the blocky, bold writing of a thriller and prominent pictures of celebrity actors, a style that echoes the film posters they are based on; he has hardback nostalgia jackets, carefully designed to look straight out of the 1950s but printed on expensive paper, and which are cooly desirable, collectable, perfect for the coffee table. Each one doesn't just sell the book in a certain way but it suggests how the book should be read. Not only that, but it is a *reading* of the book. We can see the same treatment for a host of writers who have what is known in the trade as "crossover" appeal: Philip Roth, Martin Amis, Kate Atkinson. Lee Child's covers are designed to ensure he is read on airplanes, not in the Cambridge University Library.

Most literary critics don't comment on a book's price. Yet price also affects how books are read. Price is part of how literary works of any kind are positioned (and because of how they are positioned, how they are read). Like much of a publisher's critical engagement, price isn't intrinsic to a work, yet price powerfully conditions our approaches to a work. You won't find many more popular classic novels than Jane Austen's *Pride and Prejudice*. In ebook form, you can find the book at a whole range of prices, from expensive academic editions equipped with the full scholarly apparatus to free versions scanned from old texts. Here price becomes a major differentiator, and also a commentary on how the novel is to be understood. Even at £4.99/$6.99 the work is outside the mainstream norm for popular reading. If the reader is paying more, the reader is not buying the book simply for pleasure. They are probably studying it. Priced at say £1.99/$3.99 though, Austen is suddenly in the province of beach reads; a disposable leisure item mixed in with the crime novels and psychological thrillers that dominate the ebook charts. E-books are pre-eminently price elastic and hence price is the key factor which can limit or open audiences for a given work. As an ebook publisher, it's something about which one must be acutely conscious. The matter of price is a key part of what separates canonical Austen from Austenalia. It is price that distinguishes between Austen as literature and Austen as entertainment.

No matter what the publisher does, they construct a certain gloss. The British publisher Hodder & Stoughton has, for example, recently produced a campaign called #readingwithoutprejudice. They produce a proof copy of a new book but with all the usual signifiers removed. There is no author name—for author names are probably the most significant brand identifiers in all of publishing today, a brand that is carefully constructed and cultivated. There is no cover as such, no indication of what the book is about. There is simply the injunction that we #readwithoutprejudice. Here, on the face of it, is the publisher abrogating its interpretative function.

Naturally it does no such thing. The refusal to put a spin on the book is still a spin. In an over-saturated market the refusal to play the game of author brands and to deliberately conceal the name of the author is itself a strategy. It is a commentary on how gender, class, or racial factors play into the book buying decisions of retailers, of the media, and of the public. Not only does it attract attention, but it also implicitly suggests a reading of the book. Publishers must always make the key decisions about a book's content, packaging, and presentation, from marketing materials to press releases to typography. And in making such unavoidable decisions they are always acting in some way as a critic—even when they claim to have effaced those decisions. The structure of the literary universe is dependent on a publisher's decisions.

One of the most interesting ideas around publishing is that of the Italian publisher and writer Roberto Calasso. For most of his career Calasso worked at the distinctive Milan-based publisher Adelphi Edizione. Adelphi is known in Italy for spearheading the diffusion of a certain mitteleuropean sensibility, publishing names including Nietzsche, Stirner, Walser, Jünger, Kundera, (Joseph) Roth and Spengler, not to mention authors as diverse as Borges, Tolkien, Somerset Maugham, and Canetti. There is a peculiar diversity but also coherence to the list. This is where, in his short book *The Art of the Publisher*, Calasso talks of publishing as a "form" comparable to other literary forms like the lyric or the novel. Part of this form lies in the editorial decision-making of a house; the filtration or selection of works which define the house's identity. But part of this form, as Calasso makes clear, lies in all those matters of design, format, marketing, and editing, things which are active critical engagements and outward looking interpretations.

If publishing is a form, it is a critical form. It is as interpretive as it is creative.

What, then, of this aspect in the digital world? As more text segues into digital media, publishers are going from being critics as an aspect of their work, to being critics as the center of everything they do.

In the bumpy offline world publishers still fulfill many functions. They arrange for the physical distribution of a work. They act as the venture capitalists of the literary world. Thanks to new open publishing systems and emergent new business models, both functions are, if not totally superseded, slowly retreating, or at least adjusting to publishers being no longer the only game in town. In order to be read anywhere, and to get paid for doing so, publishers "as a concept of third-party agents amplifying work" once held a monopoly. To get into bookstores, to get into the hands of readers, you needed a publisher. In the digital realm this is no longer necessarily true. Instead, all material can potentially be read easily. What then becomes of the publisher?

Take, as an example, getting an article published in the *New Yorker*. Go back fifty years and having such an article published conveyed a level of prestige. It was a great symbol. But it was also a good way of getting the words, physically, into the hands of *New Yorker* readers. Being published in the *New Yorker* was both a matter of prestige and a function of production and distribution. Now, compare this to today. The production and distribution part of the *New Yorker* still exists, sure; but its significance is greatly reduced. The fact is that having text on the website of the *New Yorker* is in technical terms much like having the text on any other website. It's hosted on servers and is served up to those who ask for it. In contrast, and as part of the same dynamic, the significance of the prestige element has been increased. Given that anything can be published anywhere at anytime by anyone, carrying the masthead of a well-respected media brand is central. It doesn't help physically with distribution; but it still has the power to deliver readers. If anything, it has an enhanced power, the potential to deliver more readers than ever.

The point is, the publishing function of the *New Yorker*, like all publishers, is shifting in emphasis. There is a flatness to the digital world that necessitates this. Every utterance takes the same shape. It's all just code and screens. All tweets resemble all other tweets in a way that all books, or all magazine articles, or even all speeches or conversations, do not resemble each other. Aside from content, the substance of an utterance tells us nothing. Only the penumbra of impressions—the branding, the marketing, the haze and fog of impressions produced through the work of media construction, publishing-as-criticism—tells us about that utterance. The communicative structure of my tweets and the *New Yorker's* tweets are the same; their power, reach, potential, and influence are not.

In the digital age publishers are becoming more and more defined by their critical functions. On Amazon, anyone can be a publisher. The difference between a book published by one of the world's major corporate houses and anyone, sitting at home, is negligible, especially with respect to those elements which physically construct the book. To be what I would call a third-party publisher (to distinguish from self-publishing) is primarily to be a critic of a work. A publisher spends time, money, and effort building the first foundational interpretation of a text, whether that means making the book ready for people to read on vacation, or whether it means making it a contender for the Booker Prize. All other elements are gradually melting into the vastness of the most open publishing platform: the Internet itself.

Think, online, of what is left of a book before you read it. There is the title and subtitle. The cover. The marketing copy—the blurb. The price. And then there is sundry other metadata supplied by the publisher, including for example BIC, BISAC, or now Thema codes, which assign subject categories to books from the highly general to the eerily specific. All of these arise from a publisher's interpretation of a book. In fact, all of these *constitute* a publisher's interpretation of a book. None of them are "true," all of them reflect how the publisher has read a work and wishes it to be read by others. Amazon is then little more than a market-driven catalog of exegetical "works," carefully composed readings of a work designed to position these works in relation to each other.

One theory of publishing posits that publishers have always been critics. Another says that they are tending towards *only* being critics. This is the impact of digital technology. The digital world assumes the other functions and leaves publishers as critics.

What a book catalog the Internet is! A near infinite, Borgesian catalog, a superabundant catalog. As discussed, we have reached the most extraordinary inflection point in the sheer amount of reading matter available. Remember: one million new books are officially published in English every year; many more are "unofficially" published. And that's before you get to all the magazine articles, the news, the social media posts, the blogs; the mind-bending amount of email or WhatsApp messages.

All of this means that, in a world of content surplus, the acts of criticism pursued by publishers when they publish are key differentiating strategies; the way a publisher "reads" a book is part of how the book finds a niche when traditional filters—such as reviews—are no longer able to keep up. Publishers, and critics are becoming part of a system to manage overabundance. As the informational/textual/

literary universe is flattened, we are left with a series of interpretations that function to position the works within the whole. We are left with a system of what amounts to interpretations because they are never final, they are always subjective, and they are all designed with the purpose of managing this surplus.

In another context I have referred to this as an ecosystem of curation, which is a feature of markets or sectors that are defined by abundance. In such a case, the system shifts towards the curatorial from the productive. Take music, for example. Spotify has around thirty million songs, all available to any user at any time. Around twenty percent of the songs on Spotify have never once been listened to, while the top 0.1% hugely dominates the charts. Spotify bought an MIT spin out company called The Echo Nest which uses audio fingerprinting techniques to create more sophisticated ways of recommending songs, breaking people out of their ingrained listening habits. Spotify hired huge numbers of playlist creators, the emerging superstar DJs of this new age of bountiful music. Yet Spotify itself is just one part of a vast ecosystem of curation that encompasses A & R executives and sleeve designers. This ecosystem includes music blogs like Pitchfork and algorithm architects at Tidal, Google, and Apple Music. The emphasis in the musical world is less about fulfilment, less about the technologies of recording and disseminating, and more about numerous different ways of managing an abundance of music. We don't think of artwork or advertising as ways of doing this; but the function they perform is to allow superabundance. The emphasis is now on differentiation—on the skill of the librarian.

The same effect can be seen in numerous areas, from fashion to food. But it's also powerfully present in the world of texts, including literary texts. The critical function becomes the central aspect of engagements with books. It is about managing the abundance. Publishers, critics, and publishers-as-critics: it's all part of what lets abundance happen.

We've always created systems for managing information and texts—in ancient Rome, Baghdad, Constantinople, and Kaifeng. And we are familiar with the systems of "search" being created in places like Silicon Valley. Yet we are perhaps less attuned to how, in a world of open and available publishing, that act becomes an act of interpretation; and how, in a context of excess, acts of interpretation are necessary acts of management, of filtering, and of positioning. This is, I believe, the central question of literature in our time.

Theory Online: A New Critical Commons?

Marc Farrant

How has the Internet altered the form and content of what is commonly known as "theory"? Since its heyday in the 1970s and 80s, theory has fallen out of favor on university campuses; most English departments consider themselves, to quote the title of Terry Eagleton's popular 2004 book, "after theory." But theory's changing institutional status has prompted a new development: in recent years, theoretical ideas have migrated beyond the academy, into new "para-academic" spaces, including the blogosphere. Since the early 2000s, the Internet has stimulated and shaped numerous new intellectual developments: new materialisms, new realisms, and new object-oriented ontologies abound online, unconstrained by disciplinary boundaries, or by the procedures of conventional academic publishing.

The burgeoning new world of "theory online" has been built through collective exchange and gestation. It's a place where tenured academics converse with geeks and autodidacts, and where social media can sometimes seem as important as peer-reviewed journals. Producing new forms of what McKenzie Wark has called "low theory", theory online appears autonomous from academic specialization, and even from the university's increasingly neoliberal values. So, are those values driving theoretical innovation outside the academy?

Or is the contemporary university, with its emphasis upon "impact" and public engagement, more compatible with the blogosphere than we might think?

Here, I trace the development and dissemination of theoretical ideas across various online platforms, from independent blogs to more journalistic publishing venues, as well as through the chatter of Twitter. Along the way, I'll explore the shifting relationship between theory, academia, and popular culture; the impact of online media upon the content of intellectual arguments; and the contrasting speeds and time signatures of academic publishing and real-time debate. Mapping the dynamics of this new field, I ask whether there's a middle way between specialism and populism, and also whether there is a middle way between "high" and "low" forms of theory. Ultimately, I aim to pose critical questions about the extent to which the new realm of "theory online" might point the way toward a new intellectual commons.

Dating the advent of the "theory blog" is a tricky task; the definitions of "theory" and "blog" are both open (or, as theorists might say, "contested") topics. Notably, theory was already "online" before blogging got started. Predating even Wikipedia, Alan Liu's venerable "Voice of the Shuttle" webpage provided a valuable hub of humanities resources as early as 1994. Also dating from the mid-nineties, philosophy professor Brian Leiter's "Philosophical Gourmet Report" (to which Leiter added a well-known blog in 2003) was, as Graham Harman remembers, one of the first sites to explore "the possibilities of the medium for the dissemination of philosophy news."

Theory blogging began in earnest around the early 2000s, and, unlike Leiter, was inspired less by mainstream Anglo-American philosophy than by cultural studies, media studies, gender studies, critical theory, and the kind of philosophy often referred to as "continental."

Blogs like the late Mark Fisher's "K-Punk," Nina Power's "Infinite Thought," Levi Bryant's "Larval Subjects," Lars Iyer's "Spurious," and others helped to build up an innovative network of blogs situated at the interstices of philosophy and popular culture. In a 2005 post entitled "Why K?," Fisher explained the motivations behind his blog:

> Why I started the blog? Because it seemed like a space—the only space—in which to maintain a kind of discourse that had started in the music press and the art schools, but which had all but died out, with what I think are appalling cultural and political consequences [...] The way in which I understood theory—primarily through popular culture—is generally detested in universities.

The excitement surrounding Fisher's blog, both on the Internet and beyond it, was summed up by Simon Reynolds in a 2009 piece for *Frieze* magazine, in which he noted that "the constellation of blogs clustered around Mark Fisher's K-punk" were written by a mixture of "practicing philosophers" and "others involved in lumpen academia (a comment on its economic precariousness, not the quality of the output, which can be extraordinarily high)."

Alongside the London-based Fisher and Power, Levi Bryant's "Larval Subjects" provided an American take on philosophy blogging, "a space," as Bryant's mission-statement puts it, "for the incubation of philosophical larvae that are yet without determinate positions or commitments, but which are in a process of unfolding." Unfixed, open, networked, and dynamic, Bryant's notion of "unfolding" pithily captures the nature of theory online.

Nina Power's "Infinite Thought" similarly exemplifies how blogging can be an incubator and laboratory, a space for informal critical experimentation. Derived from insights first formulated on her blog, Power's first book, *One-Dimensional Woman* (2009) captured and preserved the energy of the format. As one reviewer remarked, the

book's "rapid swerves from one point to another" and "brief treatment of heterogeneous topics" all "owe something to the forms of
attention encouraged by the web."

Theory blogs, at their best, were neither esoteric nor populist, and
were more accessible than conventional modes of academic writing
(such as journals, monographs, and peer-reviewed publications).
Frequently blurring the theoretical with the personal, they reflected,
instead, the different conditions of the online world. Blogs can be
single authored affairs, composed of drafts, notes, or reflections.
Others might be co-authored by a group, appearing to take the form
of a more impersonal and serious academic setting. As Jodi Dean
writes in an article on "Blogging Theory": "What the theory blogs
suggest, then, is a practice of blogging that is more than journalism,
more than diary keeping, and more than remediation."

Atomized yet collaborative, personal yet academic, theory blogging prompts us to re-examine various cultural assumptions regarding
the nature of online reception and transmission. As that review of
Power's book shows, the brevity of many blog posts is often understood as emblematic of the speed of digital transmission, whereas the
diversity and often personal nature of the blogosphere is taken as sub-
stitutive of a polemical environment, with a multiplicity of voices
and committed personalities. Given the historical distance that now
lies between the contemporary moment and the heyday of the theory
blogosphere (circa 2005), we might now seek to challenge several of
these assumptions.

Against the assumption that online theory involves a rapidity of
call and response, we might juxtapose the role of many blog sites as
digital archives, as unfolding personal or collaborative projects. As
Adam Kotsko, of the theory blogs "The Weblog" and "An und für
sich," says:

The advantages and disadvantages almost seem to me to overlap: the speed means that you can respond to critics faster, but also means you will be tempted to take less time to really ponder what they're saying, etc. I've been engaged in blog debates for over a decade now, and they often generate more heat than light.

Regarding another assumption, on the supposedly personal nature of argumentative and polemical exchanges, Harman emphasized that, indeed, blogging is:

> an incendiary, "hot" medium (McLuhan), much like talk radio. It's not the right medium for a calm, cool laying out of aloof scholarly points. Among other problems, that sort of thing works well on paper but is a dreadful bore on an electronic screen.

But Harman is also keen to qualify this opinion by re-iterating the history of polemical exchange within the history of humanities scholarship. Regarding online *ad hominem* polemics:

> Traditional academics sometimes like to call this sort of thing "petty," but their historical memories are far too short: polemic has a lively and fairly recent history in the Western humanities. I've been teaching Kierkegaard this semester, and the combative exchanges in which he was involved go far beyond anything we've seen in the blogosphere. The same for Nietzsche.

One particular area often defined by its relation to the theory blogosphere is a new strand of "realist" philosophy, denoted by various labels: "speculative realism," "object-oriented ontology," sometimes simply "new realism," or even "new materialism." Harman's Object-Oriented Philosophy blog (2009) was a significant exponent of the Object-Oriented ontology subcamp of the wider Speculative Realist movement (founded in 2007 by Harman and three other philosophers: Ray Brassier, Iain Hamilton Grant, and Quentin Meillassoux). "OOO" (as it's now sometimes known) has since become a sub-field in its own right, with a host of scholarly publications from traditional and reputable academic presses. The effects of these movements on the academy, and on academic gatekeepers (institutional organizations and journals), has been substantial. As Harman says:

> In a fringe discipline like continental philosophy, there were a relatively tiny number of journals for your article or presses that would take your book, and the journal and series editors at these venues were, generally speaking, the same people who wielded power in an organization like SPEP (Society for Phenomenology and Existential Philosophy). You had to work your way to visibility within that network, because there was no other way to go about it. And though I still think SPEP plays an important role in keeping continental philosophy institutionally afloat, its significance has been severely undermined by the new para-academic culture. This is the primary reason that Speculative Realism is not warmly welcomed in those circles.

Kotsko re-iterates this observation, noting that the influence of his blogging on his own academic career can be described as a "double edged sword":

> ...in terms of my academic reputation more broadly, it certainly has allowed me to gain a higher profile than normally would have been possible at this point in my career, but it

has also led some people to dismiss me, because they are only familiar with my dashed-off blog writing and assume that my published writings must be superficial.

The theory blogs of note and substance have been largely penned by professional academics, or by online writers who would later become employed by the academy. In fact, the profile and success of these writers is testament to the dynamism and exposure of the online medium, and how the academy has latterly sought to appropriate these forces and fashions. A particularly negative account of this metamorphosis within the academy, now largely given form under the rubric of the "Digital Humanities," might, following Jodi Dean's analysis of "communicative capitalism," suggest that institutional academia has sought to capture "critique and resistance, formatting them as contributions to the circuits in which it thrives." An alternative vision posits that certain fashions within the academy have come to overlap with online theory (for instance, interdisciplinarity), or indeed that a revived form of critical analysis, fostered online, has in fact informed the way in which new trends and fashions have entered the academy. Either way, as Harman suggests, "It does feel like the philosophy blogosophere peaked in around 2010 or 2011. It has felt a bit more dead in the past few years."

One intriguing and notable example of this para-academic discourse, that both exceeds the trope of academic re-capture and the blog format itself, is Eric Jarosinski's "Neinquarterly" (2012), a Twitter account, composed of "A Compendium of Utopian Negation." Jarosinki's para-academic and aphoristic social-media writing, arising in the aftermath of the blogging heyday, has also manifested in an alternative trajectory: formerly an Assistant Professor of German at the University of Pennsylvania, Jarosinki left academia to pursue para-academic philosophizing beyond the confines of traditional academia.

❖ ❖ ❖

If the early days of online theory were characterized by the rise of a surreptitious blogosphere as a new arena for para-academic writing and thought, a further seismic change is evidenced by the rise— arguably in response, but also from within the field—of a number of independent publishers and presses. Book series or volumes from the likes of Zed books, Zero Books, Repeater Books, Open Humanities Press, punctum, Pluto Press, Univocal, Urbanomic, OR Books, and Polity, have sought to capitalize and expand on the proliferating and dynamic force of contemporary theoretical discourse, often squeezed to the margins of disciplines and institutions. These publishers can be largely characterized and grouped by their multifarious outputs as responding to contemporary issues and trends—often interdisciplinary—by producing shorter and more accessible books outside the conventional "trade" or "academic" industry distinctions, as well as relying on quick publishing processes aided through the exploitation of digital media and resources (in terms of both marketing and production). Open-source and open-access publishing has similarly transformed the sector over the past decade. As Harman summarizes: "While I think the significance of one-on-one or group debates in the blogosphere has been overrated, what is still underrated is the much easier accessibility of articles and books, many of which are now available free of charge due to open-access publishing."

Alongside this shift within the confines of conventional publishing, a concurrent rise in the magazine-format website has eroded the monopoly—or rather, harnessed the creative potential—of earlier blogs. These sites are typical for their relative accessibility, while still servicing a narrow niche. Publications such as *n+1*, *The Los Angeles Review of Books*, *The New Inquiry*, and *The White Review* provide platforms for both established and emerging critical voices, foster lively debate, and further entrench the space of a relatively horizontal and para-academic discourse. Arguably, traditional magazine-formats and reviews have been forced to respond, as witnessed by the roster of *n+1* alumni who contribute to *The New Yorker*, or by the development of distinct branded blog pages, as seen for instance in the *London Review of Books* webpages. Adam Kotsko documents this transition: "Some time between probably 2005 and 2010, a shift happened—blogging became more institutionalized (and there were a lot more institutional blogs, including blogs from journals that tried to squeeze a little more uncompensated labor out of academics), and independent academic bloggers tended to band together into movements (such as Speculative Realism, Object-Oriented Ontology, Accelerationism, etc.)." This gradual institutionalization and normalization of the blog scene has enabled online magazines to proliferate and fructify, allowing what Kotsko calls "the modes of critical analysis inculcated in humanities graduate programs" to find a form "intended for a broader educated audience—and they have had some real successes, both in reaching that audience and in being accepted into the existing mainstream."

Online theory has become the exemplary manifestation of a critical discourse that transcends the polarization of, on the one hand, a marketized specialist culture of minutiae in academia, and on the other hand, a banal populism that has become the hallmark of newspaper cultural supplements and book pages. The nature of online theory has consequently steered a path away from the dogged -isms, proper names, schools, and camps of the so-called "theory wars" that riddled the institutional humanities in the late 1980s. Another correlate of this growing accessibility and popularization of theory has been the adoption (or re-adoption) of contemporary popular culture as a legitimate field of study (formerly the preserve and token object of a now outmoded postmodernism). This contemporary focus, made possible in large part by the digital revolution, which in turn tends to inform or constitute the cultural object of analysis, has enabled a renewed current of interdisciplinarity to flourish. Models of analysis taken from politics, economics, anthropology, ethnology, sociology, and human geography are often combined with art theory or digital and media studies, toppling the previous hegemony of theory as something exclusive to literary studies or the domain of philosophy.

Further evidence that theory has undergone a metamorphosis—rather than a decline—is to be found in contemporary fiction. The works of authors like Ben Lerner, Tom McCarthy, and Jeffrey Eugenides testify to the pervasive saturation of theoretical discourses and conceptual criticism in the wider culture. Whether or not this academic inflection within contemporary literature stimulates wider cultural innovation, it results in two demonstrable propositions: that theory transposed into more accessible forms of discursive or cultural output necessarily loses an element of criticality and rigor (not all bad), and that this wider proliferation can be traced explicitly to the socio-economic conditions of artists and writers. Access to opportunities for work in the "knowledge economy" have not only been restricted with regards to students, professional authors and artists are also increasingly dependent on the academy as a means of financial support. This is often a point of satire in the so-called "theory novels" themselves. The Nobel Laureate, J.M. Coetzee (himself a lifelong academic) parodically frames, in *Diary of a Bad Year* (2006), the inculcation of theoretical culture in the "literature classes in the United States of the 1980s and 1990s" as pivotal to the post-9/11 paranoia of American prosecutors:

> From their exposure to literary theory these not-very-bright graduates of the academy of the humanities in its postmodernist phase bore away a set of analytical instruments which they obscurely sensed could be useful outside the classroom, and an intuition that the ability to argue that nothing is as it seems to be might get you places.

More generally, this analogous representation of theoretical change in general—as one of proliferation and dissemination, away from discernible markers of institutional or disciplinary authority and legitimacy—signifies the indissociable relation of digital distribution to any discussion of the changing contexts of theory's reception. Metaphors of transparency, accessibility, immediacy, horizontality, and innovation abound; the final question is to what extent a revitalized and digital theoretical culture is able to remain critical of itself.

The institutionalization and normalization of online theory is still ongoing, and the emergence of the digital humanities as an inter-disciplinary sub-field signals one way in which academia has begun to harness the capacity and dynamism of online theory and writing, whether in order to boost an institution's perceived public "outreach," or in order to share its research in response to increased pressures to justify itself to funding bodies. Nevertheless, the digital medium undoubtedly lends itself to more youthful and marginal voices, who are not only technically more adept at exploiting the format, but who have greater reason to do so. These days, it is hard to imagine an emerging academic, theorist, or writer breaking through without him or her first publishing online. As Harman explains: "On this basis we can speak of an obvious upside to para-academic philosophy: it creates abundant opportunities for the young and the powerless that did not previously exist. It allows you simply to ignore the previous obligatory channels of intellectual maturation if you aren't permitted to enter them, or simply do not care to do so. It also introduces at least a *certain* degree of meritocracy into conversations."

The need for exposure and legitimation is as important as the need for a hospitable, collaborative, and dynamic environment of readers, especially in a culture of hiring freezes and ultra-competi-tion. Accordingly, one's online activity is increasingly understood to function as an appendage to one's résumé. There is an obvious down-side to the pressure to augment one's online profile and to ceaselessly publish: an over-abundance of available and free online materials, articles, and blogs creates a corollary surplus that depreciates cultural capital. After all, most online theory is produced without remuner-ation. A clear example of this is the rise of dubious digital publishers flaunting offers to publish work for free. With very low overhead costs, these publishers hope that by acquiring the initial copyright for work they might later resell the intellectual property rights to a reputable publisher in the event that this reputable publisher might wish to re-publish the work later on. From this perspective, the digital realm is in a position of mastery over the user. A softer perspective might position the technological revolution as a passive correlate arising directly from a super-abundance of graduate students, pushed into academia due to an inhospitable labor market and other socio-economic, generational, and cultural conditions.

Whichever way one looks at the nature of online writing, it is with online theory that we are perhaps best able to gauge the way in which the academy has responded to this shift to the Internet. Indeed, as Vincent Leitch argues in a recent work, *Literary Criticism in the 21st Century: Theory Renaissance*, it might be that the rise of online theory has not only coincided with, but profoundly structured, what he calls a "theory renaissance" within the humanistic disciplines. This renaissance is characterized by "disorganization or disaggregation of many subdiscplines, fields, and topics." As Kotsko similarly suggests: "As for influence within the academy, online trends and schools of thought certainly do get discussed— at least when they reach the point of being legitimated in "real" academic publications." This general proliferation of theory, fostered by digital forms of production and distribution, is similarly apparent in the domain of contemporary publishing. This disaggregation of theory away from proper names, isms, and schools, means that extremely popular figures, such as Slavoj Žižek, will remain largely absent from undergraduate course or module prospectuses. Conventionally, such prospectuses or "core reading" lists constitute the primary target domain of academic publishers, yet Žižek and other continental philosophical figures remain inexhaustibly popular, demonstrating a reading market beyond the parameters of traditional marketing models.

Rather ironically then, the theory renaissance is pre-empted by the theory itself; the fringe has become the center. In fact, this postmodern formulation means that theory in its newfangled digital and institutional guise is brilliantly molded to meet the ends of the neo-liberalization of the university. Disjunctive disciplines are often yoked together under the newly coined and seemingly benign appeals to interdisciplinarity or cross-disciplinarity that amount to a reduction of the constituent parts themselves. The recently introduced postgraduate funding mechanism in the UK is exemplary of this format, whereby a trans-institutional collaborative network ("consortium") is established to distribute funding across a host of regionally grouped universities. The new organization pleads the digital case for collaboration, innovation, and dissemination between disciplines and audiences, but this only masks the decreases in the funding available to participating universities. Another example of this postmodern economic model would be the introduction of liberal arts programs in the UK, which similarly seek to propagate a vision of organic wholeness and interdisciplinary vitality but in fact erode the autonomy, rigor, and capacity of traditional disciplines.

Hence the current state of academia reflects, in more ways than one, the concurrent proliferation of online discourse. While public engagement, transparency, and accountability are in principle worthy pursuits, the means to achieve them—such as through digital publishing and dissemination, through interdisciplinary rhetoric, and through restructured institutions—risk a constant appeal to the lowest common denominator. The taxonomy of neoliberal values, such as transferability and accessibility, imply an attendant subject position (reader, student, consumer) profoundly at odds with theoretical discourse: a subject of inattention and incuriosity, uninterested in specialist knowledge acquisition or difficulty. Nevertheless, the extent to which online theory is complicit in the marketization of higher education is extremely limited. If anything, online theory provides a model through which to theoretically analyze and critique this process. If the humanities are sometimes guilty of being inaccessible or elitist, forgetting their public role in society at large, the accessibility and dynamism of online theory is of a different nature to institutionalized "interdisciplinarity," primarily because it doesn't merely serve as a means to an end, but is an end in itself. This, after all, must surely be how we finally assess the true value of education.

Digital Currency

Laura Waddell

"And if there is still one hellish, truly accursed thing in our time, it is our artistic dallying with forms, instead of being like victims burnt at the stake, signaling through the flames."
—Antonin Artaud, *The Theatre and Its Double,* 1958

Commercial literary culture, from publishing to review, is in a state of exploratory flux in adapting its long-established print conventions to the oblique shape and ever-changing cultural contexts of the digital era. Traditional models of monetizing reviewing are increasingly making way for a new form of transactional flow between publication and audience, in line with digital consumer culture more widely. International digital communication is certainly possible: I write this essay in Glasgow, Scotland, for a book being published on another continent (North America) whilst taking breaks to scroll through a Twitter feed devoted to literary fiction from a third continent, Asia; but the data networks we build bit by bit, whilst both vast and numerically trackable, are increasingly interwoven and too complex to interpret when it comes to how they are otherwise valued, or how they should be valued to the benefit of intellectual and artistic integrity and the ethical financial sustainability of literary culture.

Let's say you buy a can of soda and tip it to your mouth, thinking of an advertisement where the actor, their fingers carefully not obscuring the swirling font of the brand name, iconically says "ahhh" in satisfaction. You walk by a billboard on the side of a tall building. You kick an empty pack of cigarettes lying on the pavement bearing a grim health warning with the fading white tip of your sneakers whose most prominent design feature is a bold, bright logo blazing down the side. Pushing your hand into your pocket, you unearth, amidst tissue remnants, a crumpled receipt with a discount coupon tacked on to the end, and you push it back in your pocket for later use. With your other hand, which appears to be scrolling through Facebook before you consciously realize it is doing so, you bypass a couple of ads that have found their way to the top of the algorithm (you may be female and in your thirties, but baby products hold zero interest for you), and you quickly tag a friend in a local bar's weekend photo gallery (it's a pretty good picture) whilst thinking about that event page you've been meaning to create for the launch party for the next issue of the literary magazine you freelance for. Switching to Twitter, you heart a tweet from a local food blogger teasing a recipe they've created using a branded ingredient list, intending to return to it later, as well as hearting an article on the best ways to get through a long-haul flight penned by an established lifestyle writer who smiles out from a recognizable airline seat. A friend, who happens to contribute to a review journal that still politely declines your pitches (one day they will take one), tweets about a new and interesting book that keeps cropping up lately. Hardbacks are pricy. Maybe the publisher will send you a copy if you promise to vlog review it. You compose a tweet about the bubbles in your soda; something witty, tagging the corporate account's handle, punning on their latest slogan-jingle.

The relationship between the consumer and peer-to-peer promotion is complex, and finding a way to manipulate it is of great value to corporations and media publishers. The propagation of promotion beyond traditional advertising is built into the commercial landscape of both our physical and digital worlds. One is now, of course, an extension of the other rather than them being two polar entities. Advertising exists in blatant, subtle, and hidden forms, and increasingly the lines are blurred between the promotion of original products and content itself. Advertising content is propagated through deliberately designed user experiences (such as the coolness of having certain brands highly visible on clothing) and the social spread of awareness (such as the impulse to update social media on the experience of utilizing a product or consuming media; like, to give a very simple example, by rating or sharing links). The post-purchase or process engagement of an individual consumer (of product or media, or more integral to the purposes of this essay, a media-product) may be a key part of the marketing plan. Consumers track information behind them like paw prints, sometimes explicitly and knowingly, and at other times more subtly and unconsciously. It has long been said that everyone is a critic; this is especially the case online. In the present day, everyone is also a data collection and dissemination production line, and this impacts the way in which literary media and publishing generally comes to be created, disseminated, and monetized.

Gary Steyngart foresaw in his 2010 novel *Super Sad True Love Story*, a novel set during a backdrop of international financial collapse and political insecurity, a near-future where the value of individuals is measured by digital data in a contemporary consumer society, where inhabitants display, whilst walking by electronic readers in communal city spaces, stats relating to health and income for anyone else in the vicinity to see. These stats are, in effect, the numerically calculated value of the citizen to their society, and thus their ranking within it. The novel has been described as "digital posthumanism" by the critic Raymond Malewitz in *Arizona Quarterly*. China has recently followed suit in creating such a model of organizing citizens by digital data, with access to services dependent upon a "citizen score" ranking, which is being trialed by commercial businesses before being rolled out by the state by 2020. In both of these cases, one fictional and one a modern reality, the social and commercial value of a citizen, and how they are treated or the services they may access, comes down to calculations of digital data, as well as a competitive, citizen-v-citizen model at a time when access to resources, in terms of services, may be scarce and demand high. In the UK, the Investigatory Powers Act of 2016 proposes an unprecedented level of government access to citizen communications data, and other countries have their own increasing levels of surveillance being folded into law.

What makes it all such a new playing field, of course, is the incredible amount of data individuals willingly create and store on themselves day by day, whether through social networking, personal communications, or myriad other Internet usage habits. Massive servers in rural locations and unfathomably thick server cables are far from the mind of the user who feeds into simple interfaces designed to evoke a second nature pattern of usage (social networks, when advertising offline on subway stations or in newspaper ads, may attract a demographic who are not habitually using them, but they spook the users who do so unthinkingly and often). Not only are our Internet browsing histories, credit card details, and email chains archived, but the theme of much online activity is the personal record or diary-like update. In the era of the selfie and the personal brand, an accumulation of freely offered personal information can be both habitual and compulsive. Digital webs are woven thickly, with strands linking user to user across platforms. Users may access one service online by signing into it through another, which may already contain copious personal digital data. We're encouraged to make more digital connections, or "friends," as we build networks both unintentionally and deliberately, the numbers display close to our names which are often a significant element of how our digital selves are measured—by ourselves, by others, and by advertisers looking to capitalize upon those who are prominent in a digital community.

User-generated content takes the relationship between consumer and advertiser to a strange new place. Intellectual property issues are raised in thinkpieces whenever user terms are changed on sites such as Instagram, where the terms are often regenerated after a buyout. In such instances, there are tensions between the platform, which may be free at point of use and which hosts data-led advertising, and the content which the user supplies: peer networking generated by the user (or, for the purposes of this discussion, product consumer) which plays an essential part in encouraging mutual usage through increasing connections within the platform, and emotional dependency upon the platform, the communities built inside it, and most importantly the user-generated content. The effort or work enacted by the user is that which props up the commercial framework of the social networking space, through advertising revenue, not to mention the sale of data and data analysis to third parties. It is murky: the astronomical rise of social networking and the complex ways in which data is contributed by users is distinct from the ramifications of all that data and the rights users might expect to their own content—that is, when they think about what they are giving away consciously at all. Millions of richly self-referential texts are generated on an ongoing basis each day on sites such as Facebook, and our ability to access a social library of digital biographies from our communities is subsidized by proximity to ads for singles in our area or by local sushi bars. To join in with our peers in such a social environment, we inhabit a space which requires a willingness to trade our own effort and data for commercial purposes. Digital existence, that is to say general existence, insists that we be in flux within this set of values. The existence of literary culture online follows suit. The poor life/work balance of those in the arts and with scholarly careers is both a curse and a blessing, and is already predisposed to slot into such a model.

As detailed above, contemporary commercial exchanges are no longer as simple as exchanging goods for a sum of money. There is marketing value in the disseminating behavior of consumers. The digital marketplace in its rudimentary form may have largely taken the same transactional shape as its offline predecessor in which a good is exchanged for an agreed price—but already by that point it differs materially from a physical offline transaction, replacing the process with transfers of data. A knock-on effect of this is that consumers who have turned to digital transactions in increasing numbers have grown used to paying for goods or services with some faith that the process will produce the paid good without being able to touch it first and that their financial data will remain secure. This requires a mental adjustment since one is not able to see the back end, or even understand entirely how the transaction works from a technical perspective. Instead, one places trust instead in a branded interface. In the early 2000s, it took some convincing from me, an eye-rolling teenager, before my mother would carry out Internet banking without anxiety.

Our eager obliviousness to the systems that lie behind such transactions has formed the expectations and atmosphere of contemporary Internet usage. We are often oblivious to the mechanics behind Internet use in general, where one might blog their "reads of the year" without truly understanding how it comes about that our words are formed neatly on a WordPress page but rely upon a user-friendly interface that simplifies the code behind it. Today's younger generations who have, essentially, grown up with social media have both an intuitive and fluid grasp of Internet usage and a lack of understanding or care for what is really happening to their personal data, that it may be harvested and commercialized. For many of them, it is a regular routine to upload a photograph to Facebook without considering the transactional nature of the platform, that user-generated content is what drives engagement and makes money for such sites. The lines are increasingly blurred between who benefits, or which way a transaction is weighted in the digital world not only because of the invisible and intangible nature of the transaction itself, but because despite the reams of data, the interpretive value within the system is in itself more complex than a polarized model of goods-for-service.

Brands and media publishers also establish where value lies in this complex social marketplace in a more analytical fashion, and act as a third party between user and platform, forming a convoluted publisher-consumer-platform triangle. Literary review culture emerging in digital spaces has, as such, experienced difficulties discerning how to weigh each transaction. Heavy-hitting traditional print journals retain prestigious reputations by largely keeping the same format but adapting to a digital paid subscription model. However, multi-faceted new platforms for review may take various forms but often depend upon social media to refer an audience back to an external site, meaning that there is no longer a clean and easy exchange when it comes to the procurement of reviews for money. The complex and often opaque system of values that we often ignore is a factor as much as new audience expectations as far as how such information is accessed is a factor. Readers are more used to consuming content for free but with ubiquitous ad bars down the side of the page than they are subscribing to a conventional magazine in digital form.

Digital literary reviews fit within commercial models reliant upon the audience's social engagement. Maintaining integrity in the face of the necessity to drive clicks from social media, or maintain enough activity on-site to profit from ad revenue, while at the same time paying writers or remunerating them in other ways, is a constant struggle. The e-book was not the only digital advancement for literary culture in the modern age—social communities engaging with online reviews has changed the way we do literary business, too. While the personal profile of individuals inhabiting review columns or heading editorial departments has always been an asset, never before has it been so precisely measured in digital data. Prestige once accumulated as a literary critic by integrity, style, and old-fashioned Martini lunch networking is now buttressed by the ability to bring one's own digital profile and trail of follower data to the process.

The culture of reviewing has diversified in form: book reviewers who may once, in the early era of the Internet have had a blog that took its lead from the format and style of print have now been joined by a new or adaptive generation on social platforms such as Instagram and YouTube. The slide from criticism to content may not do much for critical discussion, but it can boost sales. When taking a more personable approach, lifestyle and literary content merges, and books are as likely to be arranged as a lifestyle-signaling object in a pretty photograph as they are to be discussed in a more detailed way. Digital "influencers" can tap into target markets bracketed by age or interest. Social media is a research tool for the low budget literary marketer, who now has access to an unprecedented amount of volunteered data. Monitoring the way in which books are discussed peer-to-peer is easier online than tracking word of mouth offline. This approach can be as valuable, where appropriate, as sending out print proofs to traditional critics.

Such "influencers" are compelling communicators, and the personalized, profile-driven nature of their output, an extension of norms formed on social media, means that many also cover lifestyle topics and other products as well as books. Such informal reviewers are an important part of the book discussion ecosystem, and can appeal to audiences who may not necessarily be primary followers of book or review culture but who are led in their media consumption by personalities who touch on many topics. Followers of these accounts are drawn to them not only for the lifestyle fantasy they can evoke, but also for the sense of community, where barriers are broken down between "reviewer" and reader. Instead they can engage directly and immediately with these influencers; whether by liking or retweeting what they say, or by forming friendships around similar interests, in keeping with personal representation in a commercial environment so ubiquitous in tone to social media.

Of course, money does come into play more directly. The cozy, filmed-from-the-bedroom-or-personal-bookshelf appearance of many YouTube reviews, or the stylish flat-lay images on Instagram often do not reflect the effort that has been made by marketing and PR departments of publishers to get books there. Commercial publishers often ape the style of these online reviewers, with their own chatty YouTube channel reviews or lifestyle shots on Instagram instead of professional photography, deliberately striking a balance between consumer showcase and online community. Digital data around personal profiles in the amateur lifestyle blogging community is tracked more structurally by nimble marketers in publishing houses.

Some of the more prominent social media personalities end up headhunted by publishing houses for their flair in generating appealing book-related content and for their existing popularity with communities of reader-fans. YouTube personalities not focused primarily on books have ended up with book deals, a prominent example being Zoella who not only published her own books in a lucrative deal but who now heads up a book club in partnership with the chain WH Smith. When *Teen Vogue* announced the appointment of new editor Elaine Welteroth, they included, alongside more traditional workplace credentials, details of her significant Instagram following. Poets, writing in a medium which sometimes undersells compared to other genres and is occasionally subsidized by more prosperous titles, have made unprecedented sales by tapping into social audiences, some sharing their poetry using the hashtag #Instapoetry, such as Rupi Kaur. The balance of value may be undefined in many hobbyist fan-reviewers who are not directly renumerated for the content they create around books; but the value built into a personal profile can then go on to profit them in a more directly money-based way.

Like news and culture websites which do not pay professional writers, the less savvy are sometimes exploited. "Exposure" is a double-edged sword that can be a genuine opportunity to invest value into a personal profile, but very often it can be an attempt to gain hours of work in content creation for no direct financial outlay. To the casual onlooker, the world of casual or semi-professional reviewers may appear just to be readers enthusiastically talking about books, whereas the digital data that is accumulated in complex digital networking and audience growth, and the way in which publishers court these reviewers, as well as how some of them end up as part of the eco-system of the industry (with book deals, book clubs, and book columns), is the invisible value and sometimes the actual profit in the process. Similarly, a casual onlooker may assume that an Amazon Kindle bestseller got there by merit when it requires appeasement of an algorithm where spending money on distributing digital proofs through services such as Netgalley are followed by generating enough reviews to be eligible for Amazon promotions in the first place, or where conglomerate publishers are granted more entries to the Booker Prize and other prestigious literary prizes because they've previously won (and so accumulate chances that an indie, who may have published something truly wonderful and worthy, does not have).

This "pay to play" model is not always visible in either digital review environments which appear fan-driven or those which appear to retain critical integrity. It was dispiriting when, several months ago, a publishing house I worked for received a call from a London-based literary journal offering to write an article on indie presses if we paid them, rather disingenuously claiming that their audience would love our titles but quite unable to answer why they hadn't featured or reviewed them previously without having to be paid to do so. Similarly, an award-winning digital journal requested payment to run excerpts, a grubby mark on their integrity that would be invisible to readers. There are not only built-in inequalities in the marketing budgets of publishers which cause some books to be elevated over others, and many reviewers come to prominence not only for the strength of their expression, but the digital data and social style they bring with them.

Review culture may be more easily accessed online, but, like other digital data, the trail of money and value is difficult to discern, and, in a landscape marked by commercialized user-generated content and data-driven personal profiles, this culture will continue to evolve down these emerging paths. Now, excuse me, I've got a tweet about drinking soda to send.

The Re-Birth of the Author

Theodora Hawlin

In 1967, Roland Barthes wrote his famous essay "The Death of the Author." By 2017, it appears that the Author is as alive as the Author has ever been. In our contemporary digital society, the figure of the author has become an integral presence in the publishing process (evident in the rise of book tours, signing events, live interviews, etc.). The Internet, and social media in particular, provides a mouthpiece whereby authors are able to become a key character in the life-span of a text, with the power to continually revive and expand upon their works. Authors are more accessible to their readership than they have ever been before; even those who attempt anonymity are ultimately hunted down. Demand is high, and in this new age of digital self-fashioning the "Re-Birth of the Author" has replaced "Death."

"It's not the book that counts but the aura of its author," noted the notoriously elusive Italian novelist Elena Ferrante in an interview in the *Paris Review* prior to her non-consensual "un-masking" by a New York *Times* journalist in October 2016. Did Ferrante fear the spotlight? On the contrary, she despised it. Ferrante is one of the few, perhaps only, bestselling authors to so openly reject the renewed power of the "Author" as a character. Importantly she also identified the central problem of our contemporary publishing industry in which "the author ends up selling not only his work but also himself, his image." Her decision to remain anonymous was founded on a rebuttal of this media system, the digital "re-birth" of the author that plagues the literary world where the author's persona off the page—and on the screen—is often given as much importance as their characters on the page.

Self-fashioning is enjoying a new heyday with curated Internet profiles that mirror and bolster real-life identities. The rise of the Internet has created a convenient mouthpiece whereby publishers have been able to promote publications, and their authors, as never before. For the literary world this remains a complex conundrum. Authors—if they choose—can now remain truly present in the lives of their readers. Their existence continues beyond the page in a way that Barthes could never have dreamed. The "business of books" can clearly be seen in the online presence of an author like J. K. Rowling. The endless information that she continues to leak on Twitter about the Harry Potter books, like a steady drip feed to eager fans, provides a reliable stream of audience engagement.

The Internet's capacity to facilitate this kind of engagement and interaction is important as it also allows increased audience diversity, expands readership, and opens new avenues for books, authors, and readers. In an algorithm-fueled world where "like" fuels "like" and related content leads to related content, the ability for publishers and authors to harness this power becomes manifold. Book "bubbles" can grow large, and online popularity can be measured with facts and figures.

Yet the continued engagement of Rowling and other authors in relation to their texts also openly exposes the mechanisms of the publishing industry. "Industry" is the correct term here, as such engagement manufactures steady income, as well as steady interest. The creation of new marketing ventures and profitable projects become fundamental tools that enable an author to increase the lifespan of a text, but also more notably to increase their place within the text's narrative. Just look at Rowling's "Pottermore," a whole digital platform born out of reader demand for more information about her wizarding world. The author now has the ability to become a central character in the continual making and remaking of their own text, a figure with the power to define and redefine characters and information at their discretion.

The paper trails and private lives of authors have always fascinated readers. Yet the emails between Jonathan Safran Foer and Natalie Portman don't quite hold the same gravitas as the letters of Jean-Paul Sartre to Simone de Beauvoir. The paper-trail of emails, texts, tweets, Instagrams, articles and blog-posts has never been so thick, and yet with this excess of authorial information is anything really gained? Despite all this additional press, noise, and "presence," authors become throwaway fads, at once more palpable and more intangible than ever before. Few writers seem to survive in the public consciousness now, beyond those who remain bestsellers. An elite few attain such prominence that whatever they write sells. Review sections of newspapers are plastered with their names, if not the subjects on which they write. It's their identity, their personality, their "aura" that attracts buyers. Writers in this sacred realm can write just about anything with a reliable audience.

Those authors outside this hallowed space of fame inhabit a different kind of sphere. These writers, like fashion trends, become commodities, goods to be bought, used, sold, and discarded. In a clickbait age, fast-fashion culture is rising, and so too is reader demand and want. Consumption is high. The public is constantly bombarded by a new book, a new author, "the next big thing." These pitches often piggyback on other authors, one name selling another with the simplicity of a dust-jacket endorsement. The noise of the publishing world, thanks to social media, is louder and more dense than it's ever been. Sifting the wheat from the chaff is a whole lot harder with everyone shouting about their new rising star. Quantity is there, quality is harder to define.

Although Barthes's original notion of separating author and text still obtains, the process of separation is becoming ever more complicated in a digital world in which the presence of identity and ownership is evolving at incredible speed. Twitter followers, combined with book tours and grand book-signing events, mean authors are now more accessible to their readers, but they are also more crucially inextricable from their works than ever. What an author says in a public sphere shapes them and their works in the public eye, Chimamanda Ngozi Adichie's brilliant TED talk 'We Should All Be Feminists" became an Internet sensation, so much so that it was published as a stand-alone physical essay by Penguin despite being available for free online. Adichie herself is now—rightly—portrayed as an advocate for women's rights, yet the power of these words in forging her public identity was even more complicated than she could have anticipated. When she was revealed as the new face of Boots No7 cosmetics, the backlash online was immense, and made it clear that she needed to rapidly re-determine the rules of her identity for public consumption. It is possible to be a feminist and like make-up. As a woman and a writer Adichie should be able to inhabit both identities, yet convincing her online public of this proves to be a harder task.

When Barthes speaks of a collective place of perceptions in his essay, one could easily believe he is speaking about the web itself, a black hole in which content and opinions seem to continually spawn and then surge in popularity with alarming velocity. Yet often an author needs space from their readers, even at times from their own work. Although some clearly thrive on media attention, for others it becomes, like the Internet itself, a dangerous distraction. According to Barthes, "to write is to reach, through a preexisting impersonality." Part of the writer's job, we must remember, is inhabiting a space of "impersonality," of fantasy, illusion, and imagination. It is this liminal space that can frequently call for the relinquishing of personal identity as an essential component for a story to be told. Like famous actors attempting to shed their red-carpet smiles to inhabit a new Oscar-worthy performance, part of the writer's job is to elide their "authorial" status, to forget who they are in order to become something new. The dilemma the digital world poses has the potential to deny an author this forgetting.

For instance, Ferrante's open refusal to reveal her identity and give the literary world a solid character to cling to resulted in a violent, transgressive "investigation." By withholding her identity Ferrante became akin to a criminal. Her offense? To revoke the cult of the author and identity that so openly pervades the rhetoric of criticism in the digital age. The investigation provided author profile shots of her, images that the literary community had craved for months. It is instructive to recall that, without the typical information that an author bio provides, reviews and features on Ferrante were forced to focus more dominantly on the text. In the absence of a standard author photo, shot against foliage, publications were forced to get creative: publications from *The Guardian* to *The New Yorker* produced and commissioned some of the most interesting illustrations to accompany their pieces on Ferrante, causing there to be an almost unprecedented attentiveness to the subject of her work, not the author.

Ferrante openly named her anonymity as a form of opposition, a way of "testifying against the self-promotion imposed by the media." Curating one's digital footprint can be an empowering experience, but in such a delicate and new space as a public collective consciousness we have to remain aware that this process can also be a draining and destructive one. To establish identity is hard enough in the real world, to reinvent oneself online takes work, and not everyone desires a public identity, digital or otherwise. Sometimes it's nice not to be seen. Yet despite Barthes's assertions that the author as a figure would dwindle in public discourse, the "Author" as a manufactured image has continued to grow stronger and stronger. The cult of identity thrives on digital fuel.

What Ferrante epitomizes is the view that for most authors being seen is not the point, it's being heard. Although the two are often conflated, there's a real sense that people aren't only judging books by their covers any more, they're also judging them on their authors. Ferrante is not alone when it comes to choosing to keep her identity under wraps. Pseudonyms are rife within the literary canon. For the Brontë sisters or George Eliot it was a matter of concealing femininity in order to be published. Yet even J. K. Rowling herself, the queen of a now large and unruly publicity machine, originally made the decision to hide her femininity behind her initials on the advice of her publisher in order to appeal to a larger target audience of teenage boys. The degree of concealment was obviously far greater at a time when women were not taken seriously as writers, but one wonders how the Brontës or Eliot would have fared if the Internet had been alive and well, and investigative journalists had been able to uncover their identities? Would the literary canon be the same? Luckily for us author interviews and headshots had yet to take such keen precedence in the priorities of publishers.

The mystery of Ferrante's identity infringed upon the delicate liminal space that Barthes identified between the personality and impersonality of the writer. Her books were charged with unknown potential. Parts potentially fact, parts potentially fiction. The dilemma is that this position was not seen as an absolute position: it was not an answer. Claudio Gatti said about his investigation that "Ferrante has in a way relinquished her right to disappear behind her books and let them live and grow while their author remained unknown." Books, according to Gatti, are not allowed to "grow" without their master. Ferrante often used the image of a book as a dog and the author as a master, with a leash binding the two, emphasizing that both creatures are living things. Ferrante is clearly of Barthes's inclination that she is no longer needed, that a dog can live without its master. Gatti represents the media of our digital age that is unable to accept the empty space left by her lack of participation. To let the dog wander freely without the baggage of its owner feels impossible.

Barthes insists that a "text's unity lies not in its origin but in its destination. Yet this destination cannot any longer be personal: the reader is without history." It's clear that, for Barthes, once a text is created, its identity transcends the author and enters the realm of the reader. But what happens when the reader wants to root a text in its origin? What happens when the reader is being constantly directed and redirected by the author? What happens when the author refuses to die? When the author won't leave the text alone? What happens when the author, or rather the media of an author's image, won't let the reader take a text on in its own terms? The frequent barrage of author interviews and live Q&As often lead to disappointment, where readers seek acknowledgement and clarity that authors are often unable to deliver: they are done with the text, they have removed themselves from it and it has removed itself from them. Yet at the same time, our culture is so hungry for the author-figure. These continued reiterations and clarifications of identity in relation to a text also act as a comforting mechanism that creates a framework for the reader. Author-identities are powerful signifiers in the modern world. Do you read Zadie or Ali Smith? Do you read both? These figures, like their texts, resonate with powerful connotations. The "ideological figure" of the author that Barthes identified is still as strong as it ever was. In a sense the author has died and has been resurrected as a mythical deity, a god that the consumer worships.

In its current state we can wholeheartedly say that the writer in the digital realm has made a swift recovery. Criticism has access to more author information than ever, and with this wealth of knowledge the propensity for criticism to focus on the particulars of author influence and identity continues. Barthes's famous conclusion that "The birth of the reader must be at the cost of the death of the Author" becomes void; it is now only with both reader and author that a text can survive. If the digital age has proved anything, it's that conversation between the two continues. The world of the web is large: there's room enough for both.

Economics, Exposure and Ethics in the Digital Age

Sara Veale

I tend to approach conversations about the digitization of journalism the same way I do the subject of globalization at large, which is to say I'm far more interested in discussing its failures than its successes. As an editor and writer, journalism's shifting landscape is more than just an abstract topic for me, and I have a graveyard's worth of bones to pick, starting with the growing prevalence of unpaid editorial commissions—a direct result of the Internet's market shake-up, and a phenomenon virtually unique to the digital sphere.

While the many unpaid contributions I've made to online publications over the years have undoubtedly enriched my career—for instance, such work has helped me navigate and embed myself in the niche spheres of literary and dance criticism, and has paved the way for several rewarding in-house roles and freelance commissions—there's no denying the frustration of being unable to consistently secure a wage in the digital marketplace. The "paying your dues" line often crops up in discussions about unpaid work, implying that it's something for rookies to cut their teeth on and then progress beyond, like an internship. But here I am six years into my editorial career, and I, like many of my colleagues, still regularly field unpaid commissions alongside paid ones. I'm hard-pressed to imagine circumstances that would lead me to consider a month without pay at the company where I work in-house as an editor, but I take cuts all the time on freelance projects in the hopes that these projects might lead to a contact or commission down the road. Given the nepotism entrenched in the profession, the incentive to ignore a paycheck in favor of a potential break is ever present.

That's not to say these decisions are easy or without their indignities. I can still recall the humiliation I experienced a few years ago when I eagerly spent an hour interviewing for a contributor position at a popular online dance review only to find out the gig was unpaid. Given the fame of some of the site's writers—two are internationally recognized critics with decades of experience at leading broadsheets—and the fact that the editor was the one who approached me, citing the strength of my (paid) portfolio and going so far as to vet me in person, I was astonished to find out the site relied on voluntary contributions. The experience threw my naivety into relief, stoking insecurities about my professionalism as well as talent, and forced me to confront my assumptions about the nebulous relationship between pay and success.

You see, the mere question of why a person might write for free when she could charge for it elsewhere assumes a strict dollars-and-cents definition of compensation, something journalism has evidently moved beyond. I put this question to the editor in question, and was met with a tidy reel of stats about his site's sizeable Twitter presence (nearly 100 times as many followers as the main review I wrote for at the time) and readership (also far bigger)—an equitable proxy for remuneration, in his view. As an ad-free outlet, the site has no revenue, he explained, but his writers consistently find the exposure they receive a worthwhile trade-off.

This ready acceptance of exposure as a valid form of currency—buoyed by the quantifiable metrics of social media and their implicit promise of recognition and career progression—can be traced directly to the digitization of journalism. The surge in online journalism in the past two decades, hastened by the concurrent rise of social media, has vastly increased opportunities for writers to publish their work: the web is an ever-expanding marketplace awash with platforms, from niche genre-focused blogs to digital arms of mainstream print outlets. This increased supply of writing has unsettled prices in the industry, particularly in terms of online ad revenue, and consequently seen the erosion of many writers' capacity to command a steady wage. (As Andrew Gallix, editor-in-chief of literary webzine *3:AM Magazine*, gamely told me during my research for this essay, sites like his "make life difficult for professional journalists. We're the Uber of publishing!") Enter exposure, then, an alternative currency that online outlets can offer writers in lieu of money.

Indignant articles condemning this shifting tide abound (sample headline from Jezebel: "Don't Ask Writers to Work for Free Unless You Want an Eloquent 'Fuck Off'"). In 2013, the American essayist Tim Kreider published a widely shared, especially quotable op-ed in the New York *Times* Sunday Review lamenting the "demoralizing," "insulting" experience of being an established writer who continues to receive invitations from editors to write essays without pay—a byproduct, he says, of the shift towards an "information economy in which 'paying for things' is a quaint, discredited old twentieth century custom" and "what used to be called art" has been relegated to "the status of filler, stuff to stick between banner ads." He doesn't limit his criticism to online publications, mentioning that print magazines, students, and school administrators, have also attempted to extract "content" from him for free at one time or another. Still, he points a finger at the Internet, and specifically the digitization of journalism, as the main culprit responsible for his discontent.

Kreider makes his case against the pay-by-exposure model by likening editors who trade in hits and followers to predatory event promoters ripping off fledgling bands with empty promises of fame. Indeed, the corporate exploitation of emerging writers is a disturbingly prevalent practice—one only has to think of the Huffington

Post, which has built one of the biggest, wealthiest, highest-trafficked media empires in history by drawing a not inconsiderable amount of its content from unpaid bloggers. When asked in early 2016 to justify the practice of generating revenue via uncompensated labor, the company's UK editor-in-chief said that not paying writers "is something to be proud of," a way to "know they want to write it" and "it's not been forced." This tone-deaf response is a testament to the continued devaluation of writing as a specialist skill, not to mention a complete contradiction of the left-leaning, pro-labor values that HuffPo has built its name on.

However, while I share Kreider's frustration at "the mentality that leads people who wouldn't ask a stranger to give them a key-chain or a Twizzler to ask me to write them a thousand words for nothing," his wholesale dismissal of unpaid writing gives me pause for two reasons. The first is my acknowledgement, however begrudging, that I have in fact benefited from it. Following my meeting with the aforementioned editor, I agreed to take on a few pieces for his site and have since become a regular contributor. As it happens, the wide audience he promised me swiftly paid off, both financially and reputationally: the writing I've done under his mantle has proven among my most read and shared, granted me access to higher-profile performances and interview subjects than I was previously able to secure, and even paved the way for several new paid commissions. These are tangible rewards that don't square with the conclusion that I'm being fleeced. Of course, having a paycheck in addition to these rewards would be ideal.

The second, bigger, problem that I have with his skepticism for unpaid writing is that any argument concerning morality here surely requires differentiating between profit-hungry media firms and independent outlets where nobody gets paid—a distinction that many critics of unpaid writing, including Kreider, decline to make. "The Man" versus "The Little Guy" is certainly a conflict to reckon with in the domain of online journalism, but for every new media giant there are dozens of small websites that consist entirely of Little Guys—capable, eager writers and editors either shut out of or disenchanted by traditional journalism. I'd be remiss not to distinguish and defend their motives, seeing as I've been an active contributor to such sites throughout my editorial career.

These blogs and online magazines, particularly those in the literary sphere, form part of a bustling DIY scene manned by voluntary contributors sidestepping established channels of publishing and creating their own in-roads to the field. Some sites have ambitions to eventually grow into paying outlets, while others voluntarily operate under a gift economy rooted in benevolent creative exchange. A unifying virtue—and I include *Review 31* among such sites, where I currently commission fiction reviews—is their effort to help broaden the literary establishment's borders, using digitization to democratize access to an historically exclusive sphere and to carve out niches where there were previously no markets or available platforms.

"One of the main reasons why I started *The Literateur* was because I knew I wanted to be an academic, but I felt a bit dissatisfied with only being stuck in the 'ivory tower,'" says Kit Toda, founding editor of online literary magazine *The Literateur*. Like *Review 31*, the magazine runs on voluntary contributions from both writers and editors. "I wanted to communicate to a wider audience. I dislike exclusivity when it comes to literature and intellectual pursuit. It's not about being patronizing—I also dislike the idea of 'dumbing down.' For me, it's about access. Doing a beautiful print run of 150 on handmade paper and distributing it in a way in which, realistically, only those already 'in the know' will get to read it—that's something I'm not very interested in. Ultimately, I believe it's insular and aristocratic. That's why our name and motto [a dictionary-style definition of a literateur as 'one who is almost obnoxiously well acquainted with literature and takes care to remind you frequently of this fact'] are both pretty tongue-in-cheek. We wanted to convey the idea that it's a magazine with very high standards, with unashamed intellectualism, but without the serious exclusivity." Thanks to the site, she adds, "there are interviews, reviews and articles that wouldn't otherwise exist, as well as poems and stories that may not have found an audience without us."

Along with allowing for more voices and viewpoints, non-traditional outlets like *Review 31, The Literateur,* and Gallix's *3:AM Magazine* (also a non-paying review) let emerging writers dip a toe in the literary scene and improve their career prospects in the field. "It's not always a clear causal relation but more often a case of giving you access to a world, being visible to commissioning editors," Toda notes. "Crucially, you've had the chance to make mistakes, and had your writing improved and sharpened by editors. An editor won't be willing to pay you for your writing if she has to do massive substantial edits. But we do that—we nurture young writers if it's clear they have lots of promise. And I imagine non-paying places are generally more willing to do that.

"We also have some experienced writers who choose to keep writing for us because they get more freedom to review what they want and are less restricted by word count et cetera," she continues. "And for interviews, we've often got people who are huge admirers of the interviewee, have read their whole bibliography, so they're usually absolutely delighted to have a chance to talk to their heroes."

My own experience with unpaid criticism chimes with Toda's points. The publishing industry was still smarting from the Great Recession when I finished my master's degree, and taking on voluntary writing and editing for a handful of small literary outlets went a long way in helping me secure my first full-time job, a staff position for a small publisher, as well as the various editorial roles I've held since. I started out writing book reviews and essays, which helped me refine my critical voice, and later moved on to editing and commissioning such pieces, which was an opportunity to learn first-hand how to deliver editorial feedback and deal with publicity contacts. In 2013, I branched out into dance criticism, which brought with it the chance to further hone my skills, plus giving me the added bonus of being able to attend regular performances, to interview well-known dancers and choreographers, and to even travel abroad to cover festivals.

A chief advantage of these endeavors has been meeting enough fellow writers and editors to fashion an active, mostly paid freelance career that I can pursue on the side of my day job—a way to engage professionally with fields I admire greatly, and ones that I might have otherwise written off, given their dearth of full-time jobs.

There's much for managing editors like Toda and Gallix to gain too. Running *The Literateur* helped Toda secure an internship at a prestigious NGO—"they wanted a style guide and editorial guidelines drawn up, as well as some editing of communications, and they brought me on because they saw that I had experience of that" —and has substantially influenced her transition into academia. "There are academics I've met through *The Literateur* who have subsequently been very supportive of my academic career—one in particular helped me to get an article published. I'm sure that it can only help as well that many of our interviews have been quoted in academic books—Helen Vendler quoted my interview with Mark Ford, for example."

For Gallix, who had been teaching at The Sorbonne for eight years when he founded *3:AM* in 2000, a primary benefit of running the site has been "boosting my credibility in the mainstream media." Indeed, *3:AM* is widely credited as the first-ever literary webzine, and since its inception, which prompted the coalescence of the so-called Offbeat Generation, a collective of writers united in their rejection of marketing-based publishing (among them Tao Lin and Tom McCarthy), Gallix has gone on to secure regular commissions with the likes of *The Guardian, The Independent,* and the *New Statesman—* prestigious gigs which "absolutely" came off the back of his efforts with the site, he confirms.

Russell Bennetts, founder and editor of the online "literary-intellectual" magazine *Berfrois,* has likewise seen a boost to his media presence, particularly following his publication of the 2015 poetry collection *Poets For Corbyn*, which he "put out for free then got paid to write about [for *The Guardian*]." He's also been commissioned to speak more broadly about his site and editing at large, and even managed to parlay his role as editor-in-chief at *Berfrois* into a paid position funded through Indiegogo donations (other editors and writers remain unpaid). "The magazine is now successful enough that I can work on it full time. I'm not in any way careerist, but I'd say that running *Berfrois* has certainly helped me meet a lot of people," he says.

While these editors have all carved out careers from their unpaid endeavors, a "do it for the love" spirit underpins their efforts—the same spirit that drives me to spend long hours on unpaid commissions, which is something I've come to recognize as vital to this rumination on the tractable definition of compensation. "I don't suppose anyone these days goes into literary journalism to pay the rent, let alone to get rich," remarks Toda. "The main pay-off for me with *The Literateur* is simply the fact that it exists and can be read. And there's the satisfaction of knowing that some subsequently very successful writers had their first publication with us. That alone would be enough."

This mindset also applies to their work outside their respective outlets. "If I love another small magazine, then I would be prepared to write for them for free," says Bennetts. "Outside of writing for the big newspapers and suchlike, a lot is unpaid. The benefits are working with people I like and being published amongst writers I admire." Gallix takes a similar view: "Recently, all my book-reviewing work has been paid. The editing for *3:AM* is all unpaid. The latter fuels the former, although that's not the primary goal. The pay-off is being part of a community of talented writers from all over the English-speaking world—plugging into all that creativity."

This communal sense of creativity is not to be underestimated when discussing the ethics of unpaid writing. Kreider concludes his essay by pointing a finger at "the bottomless supply of ambitious young artists in all media who believe the line about exposure, or who are simply so thrilled at the prospect of publication that they're happy to do it free of charge." Such artists, "as a matter of principle," should refuse to write for free, he contends, "because if we all consistently say no they might, eventually, take the hint."

Here's where the distinction between The Man and The Little Guy is crucial. Is it really the "ambitious young artists" eager to publish their work and engage with like-minded creatives who are responsible for, or even capable of, buttressing journalism's teetering infrastructure? Why not focus instead on the *Huffington Posts*, *The Atlantics* and *BuzzFeeds* of the world—the for-profit websites that manage to pay editorial staff, stockholders, and wealthy figureheads, yet still call upon unpaid commissions to boost their bottom line? In 2011, HuffPo cashed in on a $315 million sale to AOL, a fortune made possible by a business model that purports to protect the free flow of information and preserve writers' right to platitudinous objectives like "to connect and be heard" while actually exploiting writers' waning market power—old capitalism dressed up as new media, essentially. Any serious conversation about how to redress journalism's dwindling wages starts with acknowledging the vast imbalance of power between major outlets like these, with their hefty budgets and international cache, and the individual underpaid writers who prop up their profits.

Equally important is the distinction between these outlets' practices and those of independent, no-budget online publications like *The Literateur* and *3:AM*—namely that the former in many cases abuse writers' ambitions while the latter endeavor to foster them. The contrast is certainly not lost on me or my fellow writers. As a colleague once told me after completing some unpaid book reviews for *Dazed Digital*, "it's really galling to see your work appear alongside an ad for Calvin Klein and know that clearly *someone* is making money out of your work but you're not getting a penny for it." That same colleague routinely writes and edits without pay for non-profit magazines for the same reason I do: because their pay-by-exposure arrangement is morally defensible. These outlets use unpaid commissions to give a platform to certain writing and writers, not to boost their profit margins on the cheap. Their lack of pay stems from a bona fide absence of funds, not the exploitative pretense that there's integrity in unpaid labor, that writing for free is some test of authenticity.

"If I had the choice to pay myself or the writers for *The Literateur*, I'd do the latter," Toda asserts. "I already feel a bit guilty that we don't pay our contributors when they give us such great work. I just have to remind myself it's not because I'm a miserly dragon jealously guarding a pile of gold but because I literally can't pay."

There's no question that digitization has greatly, and perhaps irrevocably, shifted the economics of journalism. The market value of writing both online and off is plummeting, which is regrettable. It's a complex, important craft that could use a boost in appreciation. As blogger-turned-journalist Lindy West once put it, "one weird thing about being a professional writer is that a lot of people seem to think your job is fake." It's myopic, though, to conflate the motives of budget-heavy and budget-free outlets and dismiss their practices as one and the same. And it's insulting to characterize—as Kreider and the many seasoned journalists imploring young writers "not to give it away" do—those who write for free as gullible millennials too dazzled by the thought of "elevating their profile" and "going viral" to see the con going on right under their noses; to suggest that the whole profession's problems could be swiftly solved if emerging writers were not so selfish and short-sighted.

Today's young writers are at the mercy of an over-saturated, underfunded market and are fully aware it wasn't always like this. Still, writers are doing the best they can to avail themselves of this changing landscape, particularly in the literary sphere. Some of us are students using unpaid essays to develop a critical voice. Some of us find voluntary editing a worthwhile way to navigate a field where we'd like to work someday. Some of us have perfectly satisfying alternative careers and take on free book reviews to engage with genres and authors we love. Some of us, amateurs and professionals alike, are simply happy to have our writing published without pay because we understand that passions can't always be monetized and that any chance to practice our craft is worth the effort.

It's thanks to the Little Guys that we're able to do this. Without these outlets, a great deal of excellent writing would go unwritten, or at least unpublished, and that hardly seems like the remedy for a profession in need of more respect. Criticism, like journalism and the media at large, is neither a meritocratic industry nor an egalitarian one, and while pay-by-exposure is hardly an ideal solution for leveling the field, there's no question that my generation is working hard to make the most of it.

The Essay and the Internet

Orit Gat

It's amazing how quickly things become dated online. At the early stages of my research for this essay,[2] I looked at a post on *The Atlantic* dated July 28, 2011, where its then-tech editor Alexis Madrigal announced that the magazine's site had created a category for longreads:

> *If you're a loyal follower of our work here, you know that every so often— probably once or twice a week—we put out something that goes beyond reporting and analysis of the day's news. We pride ourselves on these feature stories, many of which fall into the new Internet category of "Longreads," and think that we produce some of the best long-form technology narratives on the Web.*

The word "longreads" links to an article in the *New York Times*, published just six months earlier, entitled "Longreads: A Digital Renaissance for the Long-form?"

People were using the words "long-form" and "longreads" before *The Atlantic* and the *New York Times* discussed them. The two

---

[2] This essay is an edited version of a talk given at "The Essay" conference at the Royal College of Art, London, in May 2014. It was first published in Review 31 on 14 July 2014.

popular read-it-later apps Instapaper and Pocket (that allow you to save articles from your browser into an offline-enabled app) were started in 2008 and 2007 respectively and the @longreads Twitter account and hashtag were started in 2009. But that trend reached a level of maturity in the discussions around the term in 2011. Which seems pretty much contemporaneous to a comparable interest in the essay: the past few years have seen a steep increase in publication of essays (especially in the form of book-length collections of essays), a newfound trendiness in non-fiction (the recurring example is that Lena Dunham's character in *Girls* was not writing a novel, but a collection of personal essays), as well as a critical response to this rise of the essay.

Do longreads and long-form—those two words that developed from a hash tag—equal essay? In a way, it is instead the definition of the essay that has expanded to include the abovementioned form. The non-fiction/personal essay in the tradition of Montaigne ("some traits of my character and of my humors") as well as the long-form article, in that oh-so-American magazine style of *The New Yorker* or *The Atlantic*. Many of the conversations about the rise of the essay are related to developments in online publishing in general.

Was the new essay born online? It seems like a simple equation: with no need to regard length as a function of paper stock, the Internet becomes a sphere of infinite possibility for writing. Thus far, however, the Internet has disappointed us in the kind of writing it promotes, especially because not a lot of it was born online. Looking at the way content is organized online, it's important to note, for example, that many of the pieces distributed by services like the @longreads Twitter feed originated in offline publications, rather than longreads produced with an online audience in mind. Is print still traditionally more committed to long-form writing? And is it related to the way we perceive of economies of attention online?

The numbers are grim. Alexa—the Amazon-owned service that publicly estimates website metrics—gives the average daily time on nytimes.com as three minutes and twenty-nine seconds. It's 2:42 for the *New Yorker's* site, 3:52 for Huffington Post, and 6:16 for dailymail. com. For a sense of scale, Google tops the list: an average user spends 19:19 on it a day. We spend half an hour a day on Facebook and five minutes and twenty-two seconds on CNN.com, which is the first news/content site on Alexa's top 500 list, ranked #57, way after all social networks and a number of local Google pages, including Google Russia and Google Spain. So why is so much content offered, when our reading habits don't seem to necessitate it?

A huge part of this overproduction of content is wanting to be at the forefront of changing habits. And they are, indeed, changing. Technology like tablets, read-it-later apps, and content organizing apps like Flipboard have altered the way we read. The founder of Pocket described it as "essentially the article's second chance," improving the likelihood that it will be read—rather than just seen. Instapaper's sample article when you go to download it at the app store used to be Virginia Woolf's "The Modern Essay." I point that out not only because of its fitting nature to this subject, but also because it is telling of the ambition of the developers: to promote the reading of serious content—Woolf!—on mobile devices, online or offline.

But while technology has made this enormous leap, content has dragged its feet. The *New York Times*, for example, created the famous article "Snow Fall" in 2012—and won a Pulitzer Prize for it—but it was also a hand-coded effort that took months to create. "Snow Fall" is an essay about mountain climbing which uses the full poten- tial of digital publishing, from video to interactive maps, audio, and texts and It garnered attention and acclaim but it has also "become a symbol of the potential of journalism, but also the barrier to how something like that could be made," one developer told TechCrunch.

The fact that "Snow Fall" has such incredibly rich digital design is secondary to the key fact that here was the *New York Times* cre- ating content that was conceived for the web. True, many magazines have very active websites, but "active" mainly means slideshows, blog posts, reblogs, updates, and so on. Few create long-form content that is meant for the Internet. What do I mean by "meant for the Internet"? Not necessarily rich in features like video and gifs, but essays that respond to their surroundings—by hyperlinking, bringing up conversations that happen elsewhere on the Internet, using the possibilities of the network, but also taking online writing seriously, by paying for it, editing it, and proofreading it as rigorously as a publication would in print.

While there are countless online publications, few of them are really dedicated to taking these risks. Journalism has been making this shift over the last few years and there has been a pretty serious influx of online-based, star-studded journalism startups like at Vox Media and FiveThirtyEight. One start-up that has received a lot of attention is Medium. On its "about" page: "Through a combination of algorithmic and editorial curation, posts on Medium get spread around based on interest and engagement," and at first, Medium attracted a lot of writers and readers, yet it remained a pretty mysterious enterprise (as in, it has a brand, but no one really knows what its mission is) that basically offers a platform on which to publish long-form writing. It was started by the people who made Blogger (now Google's blogging platform) but it circulates in very different ways: they have editors who promote worthy content; they invite—and pay—famous writers to contribute; and they arrange things by "collections," so that you can follow a topic, subject, or idea.

Has it been successful? Sort of. In trending articles under the collection "contemporary art criticism" are pieces like "Banksy and the Architect: Street art is an expression of self, and so is its canvas." And "Want to Be an Artist? Lose Your Mind: Why Insanity Is the New Secret to Author Success" (complete with an image of Marina Abramović in *The Artist Is Present*). Articles from Medium do circulate very well, but at the end of the day, the site is less of a collection of writing, and more of an experiment in pushing certain content via online distribution channels, more like Vox Media and

Upworthy than The Awl. Medium tried to get out of that niche and explore other profit-oriented content, such as by buying Matter (a site that invested in long, in-depth analysis and stories about science) and Epic (which was started by the journalist who wrote an article for *Wired* that became the movie *Argo*, and supports long-form journalism online). Epic's business plan was to sell the movie rights for those articles, though the success of *Argo* was never re-enacted and Epic, like Matter, closed.

Medium is an extreme example of the proximity of startup culture and long-form writing on the Internet. It's the result of the idea that on the Internet, "content" is king. One example of the corporate style of Medium is its classification system of tagging articles by length, informing readers upfront how much time it will take them to read any given piece on the site. The time factor—considering that the average American spends twenty percent of his time online (which is about thirty hours a week) reading—points to an anxiety about having too much to read online and not enough time to read it all.

We consume so much information online these days that it seems almost a little crazy of me to call for more platforms to generate more text on the Internet. Do we need more online content or more recommendations and ways to organize our online reading lists? I would argue that what we need is a shift in attitude toward reading online. Look at the language we use: the verbs we associate with reading online, like "bookmark" and "scroll," come from the physical word of books. "Long-form" and "longread" are actually some of the first web-specific terms associated with reading that we have come up with. And with that comes the interesting assumption that rigor is built into length.

This connection between quality and length is the result of the gruelingly slow shift toward digital publishing and the presumptions (not to say prejudices) concerning the quality of what is published online. The interest in long-form writing—which is considered more "accomplished" or "serious" (but also takes advantage of the fact that on the Internet you can publish much longer pieces without needing to pay for the paper stock) is one answer. But long articles have also sparked the #tl;dr ("too long; didn't read") hashtag. #tl;dr is mockery (too long = boring), but also an excuse: it's used by people who share long articles on social media based on their title, subject, or tags, and profess to not having read the piece they are circulating (this seems to happen a lot on Reddit, too, where TLDR is also the name of a popular daily round-up of notable threads). Tl;dr may seem to stand for the idea that we publish more and read less today. In actuality, we read more today than ever in the past, especially due to the amount of information we consume online.

A lot of people tie the rise of new essayists to the Internet, but most of the conversations about the current popularity of the essay form have revolved around books, especially collections of non-fiction by a single author. But what website has distinguished itself as a home for in-depth long-form essays? You'd think the essay would be comfortable online, but in fact, it battles with the infinite-seeming possibilities in length, context, and linking on the Internet, rather than using them to their fullest. This is a result of the anxiety over the online essay going unread. You can tell how many people buy a book, but not what they do with it: if they read it, how long it took them to read, and whether or not they lent it to friends. Online, quantifiable data is readily available: it is possible to see how many people viewed a piece of writing, how much time they spent on it, and how many times they linked back to it. Who of us hasn't published a piece and then tracked how it was doing on Twitter? But online publishing allows for something else: to be ambitiously small. To publish pieces that may not travel far, but will engage fewer people for much longer.

There are many online environments in which the essay could thrive. The print-to-screen relationship is very different, for example, on a browser with countless open tabs than on an app. Apps have reshuffled attention: since you can't run two concurrently, reading an article on a magazine's app or on Instapaper is an engrossing, isolated experience that is closer to reading in print than reading on a browser.

That said, there are also countless advantages to reading on a browser: an online essay might include hyperlinks (designated with target="_blank" tags to open in a new tab) sending readers to articles or analysis that it cites. That way, reading online on a browser becomes an expansive experience, which leaves the reader with a wide network of references rather than isolates him or her as they read. There's also a growing interest nowadays in digital magazines that create personalized annotation and collection tools built into their site and/or app, which bring online reading yet another step closer to those printed PDFs we all know and love called magazines. This will also probably be the future of a slightly stagnating magazine-app industry, ever battling with the question of how to translate content traditionally consumed offline into platforms that are both recognizable—so that they feel intuitive to a reader—and representative of a magazine's characteristics. Food publishing will be at the forefront of these changing habits, with digital recipe collections and algorithmic matching, but non-fiction could follow with reference tools, recommendations, and media-rich projects of the "Snow Fall" kind.

As our relationship with the Internet and the enormous amounts of information we read on it changes, so do our publishing strategies. The new essay *could* be published on the Internet, but should it? There is a lot at stake in conversations about economies of attention online. A lot of people would be willing to pay for the site that would crack the code on how to get attention to content—and with it, advertising, influence, and numbers. The future of the online essay depends on platforms we use to publish them. It would be too easy, too optimistic, too complacent to say that the Internet liberates us from the mundane considerations of print, especially when thinking about the increasingly corporate structure of the web. That said, online, non-fiction can thrive: it is searchable, accessible to an audience beyond its "natural" readership, and open for debate. The Internet and our relationship to it is constantly changing, which means we can build new context for the writing that we want to publish—and read.

Distracted to Attention: On Digital Reading

Russell Bennetts

In his 1936 essay, "The Work of Art in the Age of Mechanical Reproduction," Walter Benjamin, referencing Georges Duhamel, wrote about the then-new medium of film and how:

> Quantity has been transmuted into quality. The greatly increased mass of participants has produced a change in the mode of participation. The fact that the new mode of participation first appeared in a disreputable form must not confuse the spectator. Yet some people have launched spirited attacks against precisely this superficial aspect. Among these, Duhamel has expressed himself in the most radical manner. What he objects to most is the kind of participation which the movie elicits from the masses. Duhamel calls the movie "a pastime for helots, a diversion for uneducated, wretched, worn-out creatures who are consumed by their worries, a spectacle which requires no concentration and presupposes no intelligence which kindles no light in the heart and awakens no hope other than the ridiculous one of someday becoming a 'star' in Los Angeles." Clearly, this is at bottom the same ancient lament that the masses seek distraction

whereas art demands concentration from the spectator. That is a commonplace.

I spoke to Legacy Russell about the continued, nay heightened, relevance of Benjamin in the age of digital reproduction. Russell is a writer and artist who was born in New York's East Village, but now resides in London's Hackney. We first met (virtually) through Twitter. A number of her performance art videos were featured in *Berfrois* before she joined the magazine as a senior editor. Our conversation began over coffee, before migrating to email.

The second interview here with Jeremy Fernando is concerned with similar themes, with an emphasis on the oh-so tactile nature of the screen. Fernando is a writer based in Singapore. We first met (virtually) through his work with the online arts journal *continent* and through his connections to the European Graduate School, where he is the Jean Baudrillard fellow and a Reader in contemporary literature. Our collaboration began as an online back-and-forth, before we finalized edits over Polish snacks on the day following the EU "Brexit" referendum.

With Legacy Russell

RB: The digital today offers conditions of distraction far beyond those envisioned by Benjamin in 1936. Can you see radical potential in this?

LR: In his inimitable way, Benjamin was calling Duhamel out for being classist. Duhamel typecasts the moviegoer as being devoid of depth. He pigeonholes the experience of cinema as base, an experience incapable of being elevated. I think fondly on Frank O'Hara's "Ave Maria" here, and his call to arms:

> Mothers of America
> 　　let your kids go to the movies!
> 　　get them out of the house so they won't know what you're up

> to it's true that fresh air is good for the body
> but what about the soul that grows in darkness, embossed by
> silvery images

This captures the essence of the life-long cultural romance so many of us have with the moving image and new media (including the Internet) as primary material. To lovingly reapply the words of Grace Miceli, we are all, regardless of gender identification, "Girls At Night On The Internet."

Benjamin writes that "A man who concentrates before a work of art is absorbed by it . . . [and] . . . [i]n contrast, the distracted mass absorbs the work of art." To take things a few steps further, the digital mass has the potential to be neither male nor female—it rejects the violence of these binaries—and is neither absorbed, nor distracted.

A digital mass reproduces. A digital mass memes. A digital mass mutates. A digital mass glitches.

My writing deals with the manner with which digital platforms allow for images, information, and data to be reproduced, modified, and critiqued in a fractal fashion. I first wrote on Glitch Feminism in 2013, with an interest in exploring these ideas; #GlitchFeminism aims to use the digital as a means of resisting the hegemony of the corporeal. Within this, to some degree, is a line of inquiry concerned with what capacity we apply "the real" as a means of undermining innovation—holding onto things that already exist, rather than investing in a future imagination. It's in the latter that there is political potential. I wonder if it was that potential for future imagination that so frightened Duhamel about the cinema; regardless, there is certainly a parallel line of cultural anxiety that resurfaces when people today disparage the digital.

Alongside this disparagement, our culture continues to fetishize print.

People always fetishize objects they can hold and touch. It's some combination of nostalgia as well this eternal desire to be closer to the artist or author. Producing via the digital does a lot to widen the reach of reading material and broadens the forum wherein people are able to participate in ongoing critical discourse. The poet and activist Essex Hemphill spoke in 1995 about "cyberspace" saying: "...I stand at the threshold of cyberspace and wonder, is it possible that I am unwelcome here, too? Will I be allowed to construct a virtual reality that empowers me? Can invisible men see their own reflections?" I think these are incredibly relevant questions to contemplate when approaching this idea of the digital, and what problems it presents (holding up a mirror to an already flawed society), and works to resolve (perhaps providing opportunities for the invisible to become visible). There's a conflict here.

We fetishize print because it exists in the realm of the real that we are familiar with; we associate reality as being commensurate with all things tangible. However, there are many things that aren't tangible that are still real. Thus, there isn't a need to let go of print, but rather there's a need to consider what else is possible. Platforms like NewHive or Inkitt have become places to experiment with this, a history that is quite literally being written as it happens.

Not letting go entirely, but is there perhaps a need to tear down print's aura?

No. I love the aura. I love breaking the spine of a book, folding down its pages, writing in the margins. These are rituals that I have built into my experience of reading, thinking, and processing.

Can't the digital have an aura, too, though?

Yes, and it's an aura always already improvised. No bound book can be (near-magically) altered using Cascading Style Sheets. And the online is more tactile than the prevailing control machine propagates.

Returning to your work, why do you believe that online literary criticism should embrace the glitch?

Glitch is ultimately a metaphor that can be mobilized across disciplines. For this reason, it is incredibly useful as a critical tool. While the word "glitch" hails from the realm of technoculture, the theorizing of glitch—especially as it relates to Glitch Feminism—reclaims the initial "error" of glitch as a term. Glitch itself is a mechanism of feedback and critique; to apply it to literary criticism therefore presents an opportunity to reconsider what it means to dismantle the vehicle of critique within the literary world. If glitch within the histories of cyber/feminisms and the Internet demands new configurations of the body as we know it, as realized via the material of the digital, then one has to ask: what would glitch demand within the history of literary criticism?

What, then, is intrinsically feminist about the glitch?

Nothing. Glitch Feminism isn't exclusively about glitching feminism, but rather about presenting an opportunity to make visible new configurations of the corporeal, with such modes of experimentation beginning online, and then entering out into the world. "The glitch" within the history of feminism is that feminism still clings to the binaries of man/woman and male/female, and so is rooted in that which is assigned at birth, not the journey that takes place thereafter. To quote Simone de Beauvoir, "One is not born, but rather becomes, a woman." Glitch is synonymous with that idea of "becom[ing]" and making room within feminisms for wandering bodies—what I like to call "Digital Orlandos" (referencing Virginia Woolf's problematic discourse of fantasy as it relates to experimentations within and across gender identifications), bodies that reject the singularity of assignment, be it online, or out in the world. Bodies existing within hyphenated identities.

Many insist on the binary of meatspace/virtual space. How does the IRL (In Real Life) critic differ from the online persona?

I take issue with this idea of "IRL" because it seems to suggest that things happening online are somehow not "real"—this idea of "real" is flawed. I prefer AFK (Away From Keyboard) which makes clearer the fact that things happening online and offline are part of a continuous loop. The constant obsession with the "real" says more about the audience than it does about the producers of content (i.e. writers online, artists online, etc.); people are uncomfortable with things they cannot touch, with things they cannot co-exist directly alongside. It requires them to reconsider space, time, and reality in ways that most are simply unprepared to.

And this ties into your critique of digital dualism.

Certainly. Digital dualism, a term coined by Nathan Jurgenson in 2011, refers to the separation of the "digital" from the "real" and those who are digital dualists believe that what takes place online is somehow separate from that which takes place away from the computer. Glitch Feminists believe that digital dualism is an artificial construct. The idea of "glitch" really pinpoints the potential for identities expressed online to be part of a process of stepping into the world at large, with a continuous loop between the two.

We're constantly slammed with the narrative of an online persona lacking accountability, that people online say things without considering impact—this would be looking at online forums and comment threads as negative spaces, or spaces inclined towards threat or violence.

The much-derided comments section.

Well, this narrative is, in my opinion, a bunch of nonsense intended to demarcate the digital as a space one should fear exclusively. The fact is, what we call "trolling" online always also exists away from the computer, and the potential for threat and violence doesn't dissolve when conversations are taken offline; people say and do harm within the arena of criticism whether they're working in the office of a top print publication or rather writing from the comfort of their own home, sounding off on the Internet.

How about the view of criticism as a phallocentric-fest? Since the first VIDA Count in 2010, orchestrated by Erin Belieu and Cate Marvin, there have actually been some noticeable improvements in the glaring gender disparities traditionally seen within the pages of leading publications. I'm thinking about positive editorial changes made at places like *Harper's* and *The New Republic* over the past few years. One wonders whether the Internet has helped to open up the game, as it were, applying increased pressure upon older print journals and magazines.

The history of criticism is indeed deeply biased, as it is co-dependent on the existence of the art or literary canon, and the idea of the canon exists within a white, heteronormative, hegemonic, trajectory. While the Internet is far from perfect, and certainly reflects many of the flaws of that which takes place offline, the importance of it is, in part, that it provides an opportunity to shatter the structure of The Critic and The Canon.

Voices that traditionally would not be heard within the realm of criticism are able to speak up and, yes, talk back. For example, offline, there really aren't many critics of color. Chris Jackson is the most visible name at the moment, I would say. However, online has given rise to a proliferation of many brilliant voices: Uzoamaka Maduka, Hannah Black, Doreen St. Felix, Michael Arceneaux, Roxane Gay. And there are many more. Via the avenue of Glitch Feminism, I am much more interested in how the Internet can help us realize new potential for that which takes place away from the computer and how digital space is political space, providing us an opportunity to challenge the status quo.

Are you here suggesting an evolution of fourth-wave feminism?

The "waves" of feminism don't necessarily fit perfectly for the periods within which they are applied—there are always exceptions, and they have always been retroactive in application—they gaze backwards, rather than reflecting the current moment or anticipating the near future. As such, they always seem to be slightly off-base. Denoting progress within the trajectory of feminism via the demarcation of "waves" allows us to clean up history, making it more linear and thus more digestible. For example, if you surf these waves, the history therein seems to suggest that race and queerness weren't part of the conversation until the arrival of third-wave feminism, when in reality there were people of color and/or queer people within the discourse of feminism throughout—for example, Sojourner Truth, a woman of color, gave her famous "Ain't I a Woman?" speech in 1851, or there's Lorraine Hansbury, a queer playwright of color, who wrote "A Raisin in the Sun" in 1959. Thus, the way these things work is, in my opinion, far more complex and intertwined.

I don't think fourth-wave feminism really knows what it is yet, as it has been named while we're all essentially standing in the center of it. Many might argue that actually what the world is hoping for is not an evolution within a fourth-wave of feminism—a wave that has yet to be truly understood or placed snugly within the annals of history—but rather an evolution of all and any feminisms that have led us to where we stand right now.

In my 2013 essay "Elsewhere, After the Flood: Glitch Feminism and the Genesis of Glitch Body Politic" I wrote about "the real problem, the core prison" being "the body itself. A body identified as female will never be equal, as the permissions involved in making this so would require male-identifying bodies . . . to systematically relinquish aspects of their privilege and provide reparation . . ." Thus, what I am suggesting is that we take pause to identify within our cultural consciousness the opportunities available to challenge the body as a social architecture, to figure out ways—via the digital, and elsewhere—to go beyond that which is physical, and to explore new (re) formations of embodiment. The house of gender and how we plan for it needs to be dismantled, and then built back up; we can't do our work as critics today while living inside it.

Have online literary journals embraced intersectionality enough?

Definitely not. There is a lot more to be done to bring hyphenated identities and intersections between race, class, and gender to the forefront. I give so many props to publications like *Pank, Apogee, Gigantic, BOMB Magazine's BOMB Daily, Two Serious Ladies, The New Inquiry*—and *Berfrois*, too! Each of these publications, in their own respect, continue to make a commitment to engaging a broader spectrum of "literary," setting a high bar for other peer journals.

Who do you consider to be the first feminist literary critic?

Lilith. Li Qingzhao. Hildegard of Bingen. Christine de Pizan. Take your pick.

With Jeremy Fernando

If writing brings with it the notion of scribbling, scribere, tearing, with one's hand, digital writing perhaps opens the possibility that it is our fingers (digits) that are doing the feeling, walking, seeing, whilst opening—by touching, caressing—the typewriter, keyboard, screen. Thus, a response to the object of one's critique, inquiry, thinking, comes through with the skin of our very fingers; where, like a surgeon examining bodies, one is attempting to see through touch, by stroking around; where one is performing a criticism through seeing without seeing; by feel. Where the digital critic is doing nothing other than playing jazz.

Lone facts are wasted online. Pessimism of the click. A click, a sound—sent out into the world. And like all postcards, one knows not where it lands, nor even if it does. But, perhaps, our fingers do: the revolution might not be televised, but will almost certainly be seen by your fingertips.

(Holy) spectre of print: fingered ink, Rorschachian stains. And, if stains, staining, quite possibly always also painting. Where what is seen by one's finger/s, typed, tapped, is always already one touching oneself onto the canvas that we call reality: where in playing this jazz, the digital critic is constantly shaping, shifting, the very canvas itself. Her canvas conjured from the absence-presence of a Nude Criticism, phallic and glitched. When, doubled-down, a closed reading spills, and where, perhaps, it is precisely in these spills—these movements that form a new, another, canvas—that one can catch a glimpse of the text itself.

The digital critic (once more): some deadened soul transmuted through plenitude. Where all (s)he can do is to type, write, feel, caress the screen, whilst doing this in memory of a pulped memory. A memory castigated in (countless) cross-referenced screen pathways. A turned blog, read only when blue. Mustering a digital language is faster than it seems. One is examining the screen tears.

Tears. Tearing. Crying. Keeping in mind that to write, that writing, écriture, always already brings with it the possibility of a cri, a crying out, or—as Nietzsche taught us—a scream. The scream of the screen. When the scrolling trigger digits once clicked in despair, are now sounding out for readers. Here: Sontag's lists. Here: Auden's screengrabbed verse.

The screen: a mirror. But perhaps never our, your, mirror. A mirror that looks back at one while whispering, I'll not be your mirror. For, as Baudrillard taught us, what seems clear, transparent, is always also potentially evil, *la transparence du mal*. Not because it only pretends to let us see, but precisely because it allows us to see too much. That it appears that we now know, can understand, exactly what happens, that the machinery has been exposed. After which, we forget that there exists a ghost in the machine, one that remains beyond us. And in thinking that we know, all that we are doing is to make meaning where there is none. A modulated distraction, wherein feedback severs (after Kracauer).

And perhaps in severing, in cutting, it always also forms a scar, a scab: what is both the remainder, the trace, mark, of what has gone, is always already done, and also a formation, a protection of what is already there, and also a potential for what is coming, what is quite possibly to come. In which the severing is what also brings forth, serves to help us catch a glimpse of potentiality. Where, what severs might well also be the server itself. A formless swell of words. And, of course, an incision. When the reader folds into her phone. How to write her into being when her very tactility comes into question?

A cut, perhaps always also a caesura. Without which, though, we would also never be able to know movement, motion—perhaps more importantly, without which we would never be able to even begin to detect, make, create meaning, never be able to read, or respond. Where perhaps, the very first cut, the very first break, puncture, punctum, is the moment where one first comes into contact with the object that one is attempting to respond with—touch as cut; with one's fingers no less.

When one censors the critic, her lusts will first burst amidst (better) avenues, then, yes, puncture. Where online literature represses, curved distraction accumulates. Electronic riverrun. To edit the bankrupt, to publish and to steal. A reproducing digital mass: endlessly generating, regenerating, bringing forth generations of itself. One that might well be the same, but—as our Thai friends have long taught us—is always also same same but different.

The digitalness of criticism. Where to touch—nay, to feel—is always already to be critical. Not just to know, to attempt to find out, but to potentially tear apart. Which is not to say that this does not come at an ever present risk—for, what might well be torn apart is our very selves.

Each existence of a critical writing bleeds the next one. To bleed, perchance to dream. For, to think, to respond to, to be with, needs, perhaps even necessitates, a relationality. And even if not that of a blood relation, perhaps always already a consanguinity of sorts. A little criticism leads away from bleeding, a lot of criticism leads back to blood (repeated after Schopenhauer, after Bacon). Repeating after Beckett? Certainly nothing to say about waiting; but, perhaps, that waiting is nothing other than the possibility of waiting itself. On the one hand, the reader, refreshing. On the other, our forgetful critic. A forgetting that parses meaning and, once published, erases the specter.

Once, a Necronaut spoke of howlings encoded like a striptease. The hidden. The shown. But, what is a striptease other than the performance—the explicit showing—of nudity while showing even more so that the one stripping is never naked. That the one who is watching, the one completing the show, the one seeing, is precisely the one who is stripped bare.

For it is not the screen that shows, but the one that is staring at the screen who is shown. Shown to be nothing other than the one who is screened. Pity the trigger thumbed digital reader. Scrolling.

About the Editors and Contributors

Houman Barekat is a London-based book critic and founding editor of *Review 31*. He reviews regularly for the *Times Literary Supplement*, the *Irish Times* and *Literary Review*, and is an occasional contributor to online publications like *3:AM*, *Full Stop*, *Asymptote* and the *Los Angeles Review of Books*.

Robert Barry is the technology and digital culture editor at *Review 31* and visual arts editor at *The Quietus*. His writing has appeared in *Frieze*, *The Wire*, *The Atlantic Monthly*, *Art Review*, *Wired*, *Fact*, and *BBC Music* magazine. After a collection of text-based musical scores published in 2015 by BCNVT of Stockholm, his latest book, *The Music of the Future*, was published in March 2017.

Russell Bennetts is the founder and editor of *Berfrois* magazine. He is also the co-founder of *Queen Mobs Teahouse*. His writing has appeared in the *Guardian Review*, the *Morning Star* and *Alcohol and Alcoholism*. He has edited two poetry collections: *Relentless by Jeff Bezos* and *Poets for Corbyn*.

Michael Bhaskar is a writer and publisher based in London and Oxford. He is co-founder of the digital publishing house, Canelo. He is author of *The Content Machine* and *Curation: The Power of Selection in a World of Excess* and regularly speaks about the future of publishing, media, culture, and society.

Kasia Boddy teaches American literature at Cambridge University. Her books include *Boxing: A Cultural History, The American Short Story Since 1950, The New Penguin Book of American Short Stories,* and *Geranium.*

Louis Bury is the author of *Exercises in Criticism,* a work of constraint-based creative criticism. He is Assistant Professor of English at Hostos Community College, CUNY. He writes about art for *Hyperallergic* and his work has appeared in *Bookforum,* the *Los Angeles Review of Books,* the *Boston Review,* and *The Believer.*

Lauren Elkin is a lecturer in the department of English and Comparative Literature at the American University of Paris. Her latest book is *Flaneuse: Women Walk the City in Paris, New York, Tokyo, Venice, and London.*

Scott Esposito is the author of *The Surrender* and co-author, with Lauren Elkin, of *The End of Oulipo?* His writing and interviews have appeared widely, including in the *Times Literary Supplement,* the *Washington Post, Tin House, The White Review, The Point, Music & Literature, BOMB,* and *Bookforum.* The editor of *The Quarterly Conversation* and a senior editor with Two Lines Press, his latest book is *The Doubles.*

Marc Farrant is a senior editor at *Review 31,* and a researcher at Goldsmiths College, University of London. He has written for the *Times Literary Supplement, The New Inquiry,* the *Los Angeles Review of Books,* and others.

Orit Gat is a writer based in New York and London whose work on art, publishing, and Internet culture has appeared in a variety of magazines. She is the features editor of *Rhizome,* contributing editor at *The White Review,* and recipient of the Creative Capital/Andy Warhol Foundation Arts Writers Grant.

Theodora Hawlin is a writer, artist, and cultural critic. She studied English at the University of Cambridge and her work has recently been nominated for *Best Small Fictions 2017*. She is social media manager for the online translation journal *Asymptote*.

Ellen Jones is criticism editor at *Asymptote* and a doctoral researcher at Queen Mary University of London. Her translations from Spanish into English have appeared in the *Guardian*, *Asymptote*, *Palabras errantes*, and *Columbia Journal*. Her translations of Enrique Winter's poems are forthcoming in *Suns* from Cardboard House Press.

Anna Kiernan is Senior Lecturer in Writing at Falmouth University. She has previously worked as Creative and Editorial Director at the writing agency Stranger Collective and as a fiction editor at Simon & Schuster Publishing UK. She co-founded the MA in Publishing at the University of Kingston.

Luke Neima is the online editor of *Granta Magazine* and deputy editor of *Review 31*. His writing has appeared in *The White Review*, the *Times Literary Supplement*, and *Prospect*. He lives in London.

Will Self is an author and journalist. His novels include *Umbrella*, *Shark*, *The Book of Dave,* and *The Butt*. He is a columnist with the *New Statesman* and reviews regularly for *The Guardian* and the *London Review of Books*. His latest novel is *Phone*.

Jonathon Sturgeon's criticism has appeared in *The American Reader*, *n+1*, and elsewhere. He is currently a senior editor at *The Baffler*.

Sara Veale is a London-based writer and editor with a focus on dance and literary criticism. Her work has appeared in *Review 31*, *Fiction Uncovered*, *Fjord Review*, *Auditorium Magazine*, *DanceTabs,* and more.

Laura Waddell works in publishing as a commissioning editor and lives in Glasgow, Scotland. As a writer, her fiction, criticism and essays have appeared in publications including *The Guardian*, *The*

Independent, 3:AM Magazine, The List, The Glasgow Review of Books, and the anthologies *Nasty Women* and *Know Your Place.*

Joanna Walsh is the author of *Hotel, Vertigo, Grow a Pair,* and *Fractals.* She writes literary and cultural criticism for *The Guardian, The New Statesman* and other magazines. She edits at *3:AM Magazine* and *Catapult Magazine,* and runs @read_women, described by the *New York Times* as "a rallying cry for equal treatment for women writers."

David Winters is co-editor in chief of *3:AM Magazine* and a researcher at Cambridge University. His writing has appeared in *The Guardian,* the *Times Literary Supplement,* and elsewhere. A collection of his essays, entitled *Infinite Fictions,* was published in 2015.